Roy Acke

Recipe Collection

Favourite recipes
~ from the best chefs in the ~
British Isles

Penguin Books

Penguin Books Ltd, Harmondsworth, Middlesex. England
Viking Penguin Inc., 40 West 23rd Street, New York,
New York 10010, USA
Penguin Books Australia Ltd, Ringwood, Victoria, Australia
Penguin Books Canada Ltd, 2801 John Street, Markham, Ontario,
Canada L3R 1B4
Penguin Books (NZ) Ltd, 182-190 Wairau Road, Auckland 10,
New Zealand

First published 1987
Copyright © Alfresco Leisure Publications plc, 1987
All rights reserved

Produced by Alfresco Leisure Publications plc, London SW10, in
conjunction with Pilot Productions Ltd, London W1

=Designed & illustrated=
by
Chris Ackerman-Eveleigh

"

Over the past ten years there has been a tremendous change in Britain's culinary scene. This book aims to reflect that change by bringing together a selection of recipes both from the established masters of the culinary art & from some less well-known exponents & young chefs, who are in the process of establishing themselves as original & creative craftsmen.

The recipes are featured alphabetically by restaurant, & the many drawings in the book will help to convey the style of the dishes.

The chefs' basic preparations have been brought together at the back of the book for easy reference, together with details of each restaurant & an index of recipes by principal ingredient. Many of the ingredients can, of course, be altered as desired, sea bass being substituted for brill, perhaps, or chicken for duck.

All the dishes in this book have been cooked in our demonstration kitchen, & I hope that you will have as much fun & excitement re-creating them in your own home as we did."

Bon appétit

Roy Ackerman

P.S.
Each recipe serves 4

Sauté of lamb with red peppers, basil & coppa

ALASTAIR LITTLE

Ingredients

4 long-cut best ends of lamb
2 fl oz / 60 ml olive oil
1 bouquet garni (1 bayleaf, 1 sprig thyme &
   3 or 4 parsley stalks)
2 lb / 900g red peppers
4 sprigs fresh basil
1 roughly diced leek
1 roughly diced onion
1 roughly diced stick celery
1 roughly diced carrot
1 fl oz / 30 ml wine vinegar
½ oz / 15g sugar
5 fl oz / 150 ml dry white wine
a little potato flour, cornflour or
   arrowroot
4 oz / 115g shredded coppa or Parma ham
salt & pepper

Method

Ask the butcher to remove the eye of meat from the best ends; reserve the trimmings & bones but discard the fat & skin.

The day before cooking, cut the meat into 1½" / 3 cm cubes, season, coat lightly with a little olive oil & marinade overnight with the bouquet garni.

Wash the red peppers, dry them, then grill or fry them to facilitate removal of the skin.

When cool remove the skin & seeds & cut into 1" / 2 cm dice.

Marinade overnight with a little salt, a few chopped basil leaves & some olive oil.

For the stock, brown the lamb bones in an oven preheated to 350°F / 180°C / gas 4, then drain off the fat.

In a large saucepan fry the diced vegetables until golden, add the lamb bones, deglaze the pan with the wine vinegar & sugar, then just cover the bones with water.

Boil rapidly until the liquid has reduced almost completely, cover with water again & simmer for 2 hours, skimming occasionally, until reduced by three-quarters.

To cook the lamb, heat a frying pan, brown the lamb pieces evenly & transfer them to a casserole.

Deglaze the pan with the white wine, then add the liquid to the casserole.

Add the bouquet garni, cover & simmer very slowly for 1½ hours, ensuring that the liquid does not evaporate.

When cooked, drain the juices from the casserole into the stock, bring to the boil, skim, season & thicken with a little potato flour, cornflour or arrowroot.

Add the meat to this sauce, reheat gently, then add the ham.

Reheat the peppers in a frying pan & serve the lamb with the peppers in soup plates, scattered with the rest of the shredded basil leaves.

Hawthorn & cucumber soup

ALTNAHARRIE INN
Gunn Eriksen

Ingredients

35 fl oz / 1 ltr pigeon stock (see page 150)
2 oz / 60g onion
6 oz / 170g potato
1 pt / 500 ml young, freshly picked hawthorn
  leaves
1 roughly diced large cucumber
5 fl oz / 150 ml double cream
a little lemon juice
nutmeg
salt & pepper
hawthorn leaves & flowers for garnish

Method

Make a pigeon stock, adding the onion &
potato to flavour & thicken.
  Add the hawthorn leaves & simmer for 2-3
minutes; mix in the cucumber, liquidise,
then pass through a sieve.
  Add the cream, season to taste with the
lemon juice, the nutmeg, salt & pepper &
reheat.
  Ensure that the soup does not boil as the
cucumber must remain almost raw.
  Garnish with hawthorn leaves & flowers &
serve at once.

  This recipe was devised one day when some
guests had been staying at the Inn for
quite a long time & ideas were running low.
Gunn was walking in the garden & came
across a beautiful hawthorn bush all in
flower & thought — why not?

Brill in a bittercress & white Burgundy sauce

Ingredients

2 small brill
1 oz / 30g butter
2 oz / 60g finely chopped onion
5 fl oz / 150 ml milk
1 handful bittercress
6 fl oz / 180 ml white Burgundy
salt & pepper

Method

Fillet & skin the brill, make a stock from the bones (see page 151) & reduce to 3 fl oz / 90ml.

Melt half the butter in a saucepan & gently sauté the onion; add the milk & cook until the onion is soft.

Add the bittercress, remove from the heat & liquidise.

Return to the heat, pour in the fish stock & two-thirds of the wine & season to taste.

Meanwhile, season the brill, poach lightly in the remaining wine & butter, then drain.

Pour the sauce on to 4 warmed plates & place a brill fillet on each.

Decorate with a bunch of bittercress & serve at once.

Bittercress is a plant that most people know only as a garden pest. This recipe is quite delicious, & is a great way to enjoy this weed.

Gratin de pamplemousse rose

L'ARLEQUIN
Christian Delteil

Ingredients

4 egg yolks
1 tbsp grapefruit juice
2 oz / 60g castor sugar
3 tsp whipping cream
4 pink grapefruit, cut into segments

Method

Put the egg yolks, grapefruit juice & sugar in a basin & whisk continuously over hot water until the mixture thickens.

Remove from the heat & add the cream.

Arrange the grapefruit segments in a rosette on 4 plates, coat lightly with the sabayon & place under a hot grill.

Glaze until the sabayon is golden-brown & serve at once.

Jardinière de langoustines

Ingredients

Ratatouille
4 fl oz / 120ml olive oil
2oz / 60g very finely chopped onion
1 crushed clove garlic
4oz / 115g very finely diced red pepper
4oz / 115g peeled, seeded & diced tomato
4oz / 115g very finely diced courgette
4oz / 115g very finely diced aubergine
salt & pepper

Langoustines
24 langoustine tails
1 lightly beaten egg white
1 tbsp cornflour

To serve
4 portions mesclun salad
2 fl oz / 60 ml vinaigrette

Method

For the ratatouille, heat half the oil in a small saucepan, add the onion, garlic & red pepper & cook gently until just soft; add the tomato & cook for 5 minutes.

Meanwhile, fry the courgette & aubergine briefly in the remaining oil, add to the other ingredients, season to taste & simmer for 5 minutes.

For the langoustines, peel them, dip into the egg white, dust with cornflour & mix by hand so that they are evenly coated with the batter.

Deep-fry in hot oil until golden-brown.

To serve, dress the mesclun salad & arrange on 4 plates, surround with the ratatouille, top with the hot langoustine tails & serve at once.

Sauté of calves' liver with whiskey & tarragon

BALLYMALOE HOUSE
Myrtle Allen

Ingredients.

2 oz / 60g butter
4 slices calves' liver, each 6 oz / 170g
1 oz / 30g flour
3 fl oz / 90ml whiskey
8 fl oz / 240ml good stock (see page 150)
garlic to taste
1 tbsp chopped tarragon leaves
5 fl oz / 150ml double cream
salt & pepper

Method

Heat the butter in a heavy frying pan until foaming.

Season the liver & coat in the flour, shaking off any excess.

Fry on both sides, then push the meat to one side of the pan.

Pour in the whiskey & either tilt the pan to ignite if cooking by gas or else light with a match.

When the flames have died down add the stock, garlic & tarragon.

Reduce until slightly thickened, add the cream, reduce to a coating consistency & serve at once.

Tomato & fresh crab ring

Ingredients

1 lb / 450g ripe tomatoes, peeled, halved &
  seeded
1 spring onion or 1oz / 30g chopped onion
2 sprigs basil
2 tsp white wine vinegar
1 tsp salt
1 tsp sugar
freshly ground black pepper
1/2 oz / 15g gelatine

Filling

1 lb / 450g mixed crab meat
4 fl oz / 115g mayonnaise
1/4 tsp very finely grated onion
salt & pepper

Method

Purée the tomatoes with the onion, 1
sprig of basil, the vinegar, salt, sugar &
pepper in a blender or food processor.

Finely chop the remaining basil leaves.

Pass the purée through a sieve, add the
chopped basil leaves & make up to 1pt / 500ml
with a little water, if necessary.

Dissolve the gelatine in a little warm
water, add to the purée, then pour into a
ring mould & refrigerate for at least 2
hours.

For the filling, mix the crab meat with
the mayonnaise & onion, then season to
taste.

Unmould the tomato ring by dipping the
mould briefly in warm water & turning out
on to a serving plate.

Fill the centre of the ring with the crab
mixture & garnish, if desired, with
lettuce, watercress, chicory or avocado.

Paupiettes of veal stuffed with chicken & sage mousse

Bodysgallen Hall

Peter Leggat

Ingredients

6 oz / 170 g breast of chicken
1 egg white
1 dssp freshly chopped sage leaves
3 fl oz / 90 ml double cream
4 escalopes of veal, each 4 oz / 115 g
salt & pepper

Sauce

1 oz / 30 g butter
2 oz / 60 g finely chopped onion
chopped leaves of 1 sprig thyme
chopped leaves of 2 sprigs basil

4 fl oz / 120 ml sieved tomato
3 fl oz / 90 ml double cream
Garnish & cooking
3 oz / 90g butter
8 oz / 225g leeks

Method

Put the chicken, egg white & sage into a blender & blend to a purée.

Put the purée into a clean bowl, gradually beat in the cream & season with salt & pepper.

Spread this mousse evenly over each of the escalopes, then carefully roll them up.

Secure with cocktail sticks, or tie at each end to retain the shape.

For the sauce, melt the butter in a saucepan, add the onion & herbs & cook until soft.

Add the tomato, simmer for 10 minutes, add the cream, reboil, then pass through a strainer into a clean pan.

Season with salt & pepper, & keep hot.

To cook, melt 2oz / 60g butter in a frying pan, & when hot season the paupiettes with salt & pepper & lay them in the pan.

Cook gently for about 5 minutes, turning frequently, then put them into an oven preheated to 350°F / 180°C / gas 4. Cook for 10-15 minutes - they should be firm to the touch.

Meanwhile cut the leeks into fine strips about 1½" / 3cm long. Melt the remaining 1oz / 30g butter in a frying pan & cook the leeks gently, seasoned with salt & pepper, keeping them slightly crisp.

When the paupiettes are cooked slice them into rondels, cover the base of each plate with the tomato sauce, arrange a bed of leeks in the centre & lay the sliced paupiettes on top.

Serve immediately.

Roast chicken with tarragon, brandy & cream

Joyce Molyneux
CARVED ANGEL

Ingredients

2 oz / 60 g butter
2 tbsp chopped tarragon
1 roasting chicken, 3½ - 4 lb / 1.5 - 1.75 kg
2 tbsp brandy
1 dssp flour
10 fl oz / 300 ml chicken stock (see page 148)
5 fl oz / 150 ml cream
salt & pepper

Method

Soften the butter & mix in the tarragon.

Using your fingers, loosen the skin on the breast of the chicken, starting at the pointed end of the breast bone.

Gently lift the skin along the breast & over the tops of the legs.

Put the softened butter between the skin & flesh of the exposed areas, then spread out, using the skin to flatten the butter.

Season inside.

Tie the chicken to retain a good shape, brush with melted butter & cook in an oven preheated to 375°F / 190°C / gas 5 for 20 minutes.

Baste with the cooking juices, then reduce heat to 325°F / 170°C / gas 3.

Cook for a further hour, basting every 20 minutes.

To test whether the chicken is cooked, insert a needle or fine skewer into the thick part of the leg - if the juices run clear, it is ready.

Remove from the oven & pour off the surplus butter, keeping the juices & a little butter for making the sauce.

Place the pan on top of the cooker, pour the brandy over the chicken & set alight.

When the flames have subsided, place the chicken on a serving dish & keep hot.

Sprinkle the flour into the roasting tin & stir into the juices.

Add the chicken stock & cream.

Cook for a few minutes, season to taste & strain into a sauceboat.

Carve the chicken, & hand the sauce separately.

Crab soufflé suissesse

CARVED ANGEL
Joyce Molyneux

Ingredients

1 oz / 30g butter
1 oz / 30g flour
8 fl oz / 240 ml fish stock
       (see page 151)
2 oz / 60g brown crab meat
2 oz / 60g white crab meat
a little lemon juice
1 tsp tomato purée
1 dssp sherry
3 eggs, separated
10 fl oz / 300 ml double cream
2 oz / 60g freshly grated parmesan
salt & pepper

Method

Melt the butter in a saucepan, add the flour, cook for a few minutes, stirring frequently, then gradually add the fish stock.

Cook gently for 10 minutes, then remove from the heat & cool.

Add the crab meat, season & sharpen with lemon juice.

Add the tomato purée, sherry & egg yolks & mix well.

Whip the whites stiffly & fold into the crab mixture.

Pour into a greased 2 pt / 1 ltr ring mould.

Cook in a bain-marie in an oven preheated to 375 °F / 190 °C / gas 5 until set, then remove from the oven & cool slightly.

Turn out on to an ovenproof serving dish.

Pour over the cream, sprinkle with parmesan & bake in the oven at the same temperature as before for about 15 minutes.

Serve immediately.

Lemon & coconut cream

Ingredients

grated rind & juice of 2 lemons
4 oz / 115 g sugar
3 eggs
1 oz / 30 g butter
2 oz / 60 g grated creamed coconut

Method

Put all the ingredients in a basin & cook in a bain-marie on top of the stove, stirring continuously until the mixture thickens.

Serve in meringue nests, in sweet pastry cases or with langues de chat.

Dublin Bay prawns with garlic & herb butter

CELLAR RESTAURANT
Peter Jukes

Ingredients

1 lb / 450g unsalted butter
2 crushed cloves garlic
½ tsp mustard powder
½ tsp curry powder
1 tbsp fresh, finely chopped herbs (parsley, chervil or tarragon)
4 lb / 2 kg fresh raw Dublin Bay prawns
seasalt to taste

Method

Blend the butter with the flavourings & herbs & refrigerate until hard.

Bring to the boil a pot of water large enough for the prawns not to be crushed, add the seasalt & plunge in the live prawns for about 60 seconds.

Remove & drain well, then place in a deep baking dish with the hard herb butter.

Bake in an oven preheated to 375°F / 190°C / gas 5 for 5-10 minutes.

When the butter is sizzling remove the tray from the oven, put the whole prawns on 4 hot plates & pour over the hot herb butter.

Serve at once with plenty of good bread, a large bowl of tossed salad & copious amounts of chilled white wine.

This dish is ideal for alfresco eating, preferably with your fingers, & the quantities given are for a feast-sized main course.

Haddock & crab en croûte

Ingredients

12 oz / 340g mixed crab meat
1 tsp chopped tarragon & chervil
juice of 1 lemon
4 skinned & boned haddock fillets, each
  weighing 5 oz / 145g
12 oz / 340g puff pastry (see page 152)
1 egg for egg wash
salt & pepper

Method

Mix together the crab meat, herbs, lemon juice & seasoning.

Lay the haddock fillets flat, skinned side up, divide the crab mixture into 4, spread over the thick part of each fillet & fold the tail end over the stuffing.

Roll out the puff pastry to a thickness of 1/16"/2mm & divide into 4 trim rectangles.

Place one haddock portion on each piece of pastry, fold the pastry over completely to make a parcel & egg-wash the joins.

Place the parcels on a flat, greased baking tray with the joins underneath, then egg-wash the tops.

Bake in an oven preheated to 400°F / 200°C / gas 6 for about 20 minutes, until the pastry is golden-brown.

Remove from the oven, cut each parcel in half, pull the halves apart slightly to display the filling & serve at once.

A tomato coulis, hollandaise sauce or cheese sauce would go well with this dish.

CHEZ NOUS

LA CUISINE SPONTANÉE

Confit de canard au chou vert et aux pignons de pin

CHEZ NOUS
Jacques Marchal

Ingredients

4 duck legs
concentrated duck stock (see method)
1 savoy cabbage
walnut oil French dressing
2 oz / 60g pine kernels
salt

Method

If you buy whole ducks, remove the legs & breasts, reserving the breasts for another dish.

Make a stock from the duck carcasses & reduce by boiling until it is very concentrated.

Put the duck legs on a roasting tray & cook in an oven preheated to 325°F / 170°C / gas 3 for about 90 minutes until very well cooked — the meat should fall from the bones.

Remove from the oven & cool slightly.

Remove the bones from the legs &, keeping the meat intact, place it in an earthenware jar.

Pour the fat & cooking juices over the duck & leave in a cool place — not the refrigerator — for a few days before use.

When you want to serve the dish, wash the cabbage & cut into thin strips.

Prepare a steamer, or set a colander over boiling water.

Remove the duck from the jar & brown quickly on all sides, preferably in a non-stick pan, then add the concentrated stock.

Meanwhile, season the cabbage with a little salt, place in the steamer or colander, cover with a lid & steam quickly for a couple of minutes, keeping it slightly crisp.

Drain the cabbage & dress with the walnut oil vinaigrette. Add the pine kernels.

Place the cabbage on plates & arrange the duck on top.

Serve immediately.

Tronçons de lotte rôtis au coulis de poivrons doux

CHEZ NOUS
Jacques Marchal

Ingredients

2oz / 60g butter
4oz / 115g finely chopped onion or shallot
1 red pepper

1½ lb / 680g boned 8 skinned monkfish tails
2½ fl oz / 75 ml dry white wine
5 fl oz / 150 ml fish stock (see page 151)
4 fl oz / 120 ml double cream
salt 8 cayenne pepper
1 tsp chopped chives for garnish

Method

Melt the butter in a small pan 8 add the finely chopped onion or shallot.

Cook gently until soft, remove half the mixture 8 put on to a baking tray ready to cook the fish.

Wash 8 cut the pepper, remove seeds 8 chop finely.

Add to the softened onion in the pan, cover 8 cook gently until soft, stirring frequently.

Meanwhile, season the fish with salt 8 cayenne pepper 8 place on top of the onion/shallot mixture on the baking tray.

Bake in an oven preheated to 350°F / 180°C / gas 4 for about 10 minutes.

When the pepper has softened, blend to a purée in a food processor.

When the fish is cooked, remove from the oven 8 pour off the juices into a clean saucepan. Keep the fish warm whilst making the sauce.

Add the white wine 8 fish stock to the pan 8 boil until reduced by half.

Add the cream 8 bring back to the boil, allowing the sauce to reduce to a creamy consistency.

Stir in the red pepper purée, simmer for

a few minutes 8 strain into a clean pan.

To serve, coat each plate with some of the sauce, slice the fillets of fish 8 arrange on top of the sauce.

Sprinkle with chopped chives.

Gâteau aux amandes et au chocolat aux deux sauces

CHEZ NOUS
Jacques Marchal

Ingredients

4oz / 115g ground almonds
1½ oz / 45g self - raising flour
1 oz / 30g cocoa powder
4oz / 115g castor sugar
4 eggs, separated

Mousse
4oz / 115g butter
4oz / 115g dark chocolate
4 eggs, separated

Sauces
1pt / 500ml milk
4oz / 115g castor sugar
4 egg yolks
few drops vanilla essence
1 dssp instant coffee powder

Method

For the gâteau, sieve the ground almonds,
flour & cocoa powder into a bowl with the
castor sugar
  Add the egg yolks & mix briefly.

Beat the egg whites until stiff but not dry, then carefully fold them into the mixture.

Spread on to a greased Swiss roll tin & bake for 5 minutes in an oven preheated to 375°F / 190°C / gas 5 – it is cooked when springy to the touch.

Remove from the tin when cooked, & cool on a wire tray.

For the mousse, melt the butter & chocolate in a basin over hot water.

Lightly beat the egg yolks & add the melted butter & chocolate to them.

Beat the egg whites until stiff but not dry, carefully fold them into the mixture, then chill in the refrigerator.

For the sauces, put the milk into a saucepan & heat to just below boiling point.

Whisk the sugar & egg yolks in a basin until light & smooth & gradually pour on the milk, whisking continuously.

Return to the saucepan & cook gently, stirring all the time with a wooden spoon.

The mixture will thicken slightly & just coat the back of a spoon – do not boil.

Pour half the sauce into a bowl & add the vanilla essence to it. Add the coffee to the other half. Allow both to cool.

When the mousse is set & the cake cold, trim off the hardened edges of the cake & cut lengthwise into 3 equal slices.

Sandwich these together with layers of mousse, then cover the top & sides with mousse.

Chill in the refrigerator for 2-3 hours.

To serve, coat the bottom of a large plate half with vanilla sauce & half with coffee sauce, cut 2 slices of gâteau and lay one on each sauce (ie 2 per plate).

Decorate with sprigs of fresh mint, if desired.

Serves 8.

Jacques Marchal likes to add a spoonful of home-made chestnut ice-cream to this dish.

Fillet of lamb with fresh mint cream sauce

CLARIDGE'S
Marjan Lesnik

Ingredients

4 best ends of lamb
10 fl oz / 300ml jus lié made with the lamb
   bones (see page 149)
1 fl oz / 30ml cooking oil
4oz / 115g butter
6 finely chopped shallots
1 bunch mint
8 fl oz / 240ml dry white wine
10 fl oz / 300ml double cream
16 boiled small new potatoes
salt & pepper

CLARIDGE'S

Method

Ask the butcher to remove the eye of the meat; reserve the trimmings & bones but discard the fat & skin.

Use the bones to make the jus lié well in advance.

Heat the oil in a frying pan, season the lamb fillets & cook as desired — they are best kept just pink.

Remove to a hot dish & keep warm.

Pour the oil away & in the pan heat half the butter.

Add the shallots, the meat trimmings & half the mint, roughly chopped.

Fry for a few minutes, pour in the white wine & reduce to a syrupy consistency.

Add the jus lié & reduce to a coating consistency.

Strain half the sauce into a clean pan & keep hot.

Reserve the 8 best mint leaves for the garnish & add the remainder to the other half of the sauce.

Simmer to extract the flavour, add the cream & cook gently for a few minutes.

Strain into a clean pan & whisk in the remaining butter.

To serve, coat 4 plates with a layer of the cream sauce, slice the lamb thinly & arrange on the sauce.

Lightly coat the lamb with the brown sauce, garnish with the new potatoes & mint leaves & serve immediately.

Pigeon breasts with red wine bacon & foie gras

CORSE LAWN
Baba Hine

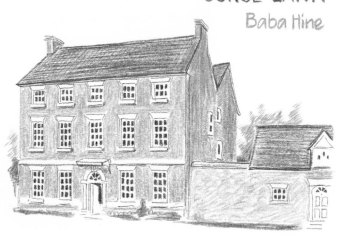

Ingredients

4 pigeons
1 roughly diced medium onion
2 roughly diced leeks
2 roughly diced carrots
1 roughly diced stick celery
1 bouquet garni (parsley stalks, thyme & bay leaf)
3oz / 85g butter
a little oil
4 diced rashers bacon
4 slices fresh foie gras
5 fl oz / 150 ml red wine
1pt / 500ml stock (see method)
parsley to garnish
salt & pepper

Method

Remove the breasts from the pigeons & skin them.

Chop the legs & carcasses of the pigeons & fry with the vegetables & bouquet garni in half the butter.

Cover with 1½ pt / 750 ml cold water, bring to the boil, simmer for 1½ hours to produce a good stock, strain & reserve.

Heat a frying pan, add 1oz / 30g butter & a little oil, season the pigeon breasts & add to the pan with the bacon.

Cook the breasts for about 3-4 minutes each side — they should be pink in the middle - remove from the pan with the bacon & keep warm.

In a separate pan, fry the slices of foie gras quickly in the remaining butter, remove from the pan & keep warm.

Deglaze the pans in which the pigeon breasts & foie gras were cooked with the red wine, reduce by half, then add the stock & boil until reduced to a syrupy consistency.

Slice the pigeon breasts, arrange on a plate with the foie gras & bacon, & pour the sauce around.

Garnish with parsley.

Paupiettes of wild rabbit with lovage & mustard

CROQUE-EN-BOUCHE
Marion Jones

Ingredients

2 young wild rabbits
Marinade
2 tbsp white wine
4 tbsp olive oil
juice of 1 lemon
Stuffing
1 small onion
1 clove garlic
1½ oz / 45g butter
1 heaped tbsp breadcrumbs
1 egg yolk
6 young lovage stems about 8"/ 20cm high
Cooking
2 tbsp Dijon mustard
1 fl oz / 30 ml oil
1oz / 30g butter
2 tbsp Calvados
10 fl oz / 300 ml light stock (see page 148)
5 fl oz / 150 ml double cream
salt & black pepper

Method

The day before cooking, separate the haunches of the rabbits by cutting just behind the shoulders.
Cut down each side of the backbone, separate the back legs from the carcass & bone them out.

Mix the marinade ingredients together, season with salt & pepper, & pour over the rabbit, turning occasionally.

Use the shoulder & other bones to make a light stock.

For the stuffing, finely chop the onion & garlic, cook in butter until soft, then mix with the crumbs & seasoning.

When cool, add the egg yolk & chopped lovage leaves.

Chop the lovage stalks & reserve.

To cook, drain the rabbit pieces on kitchen paper, spread them out & coat lightly inside with half the mustard.

Divide the stuffing between the pieces, fold over & tie with string.

Heat a flameproof dish on top of the stove, add the oil & butter & quickly brown the rabbit parcels, turning frequently.

Remove from the heat, season with salt & black pepper, flame with Calvados, pour over the stock & add the chopped lovage stems.

Lift the pieces on to a wire rack across the dish, leaving the stock underneath, & place in an oven preheated to 425°F / 220°C / gas 7.

Cook for 10 minutes each side, basting with stock at least twice during this time.

When cooked, remove from the oven & keep warm.

For the sauce, strain the cooking juices into a small pan, add the cream & the remaining mustard, & reduce to a coating consistency.

To serve, remove the strings, cut each paupiette into 5 or 6 small slices & arrange on a large dish.

Strain the sauce, pour over the slices & decorate with small lovage leaves.

Note: if lovage is not available, marjoram is an excellent substitute.

Auld Alliance ice-cream

Ingredients

THE CROSS, KINGUSSIE
Ruth Hadley

12 oz / 340g Agen prunes
2 large eggs
6 oz / 170g sugar
6 tbsp water
10 fl oz / 300 ml double cream
2 fl oz / 60ml whisky

Garnish

8 whole stoned prunes soaked in whisky

Method

Soak the prunes in cold water, then cook gently until soft.

Remove the stones, purée the prunes, sieve if desired & allow to cool.

Whisk the eggs in a basin until frothy.

Dissolve the sugar in the water, bring to the boil, & boil without stirring for 3 minutes.

Pour the syrup over the eggs, whisking all the time until the mixture thickens.

Whisk in the fruit purée.

Whisk the cream until thick & fold into the mixture with the whisky.

Pour into a mould & freeze - there is no need to stir during freezing.

To serve, turn out of the mould, slice & garnish each portion with a whole stoned prune.

Serves 8.

Breast & leg of pheasant with green peppercorns

Ingredients

1 large cleaned & sliced leek
2 pheasants, the legs & breasts removed
1 pt / 500ml pheasant stock (see page 148)
5 fl oz / 150 ml white wine
4 large cabbage leaves
1 oz / 30g butter
1 oz / 30g green peppercorns
5 fl oz / 150 ml double cream
salt & pepper

Method

Put the leek in a casserole, place the pheasant legs on top, season, cover with half the stock & half the wine & braise slowly until tender in an oven preheated to 350°F / 180°C / gas 4 for 45 minutes.

Take the leg meat off the bones & chop roughly, reduce the cooking liquid & leeks to 6 fl oz / 180 ml, then add to the leg meat.

Blanch the cabbage leaves in boiling water for 3-4 minutes, refresh in cold, drain well & use to line 4 ramekins.

Divide the leg meat & leeks between them, fold the leaves over the top, seal with aluminium foil & bake in a bain-marie at the same temperature for about 25 minutes.

Skin the breasts, season, sauté quickly in hot butter to seal, then transfer to the oven for 10-12 minutes until just cooked.

Deglaze the pan with the remaining wine, add the rest of the stock, reduce by half, add the green peppercorns & cream & reduce to a coating consistency.

To serve, turn out the cabbage ramekins on to 4 hot plates, slice the breasts & fan out around the cabbage, coat with the sauce & serve at once.

Fillets of red mullet with vinaigrette

THE DORCHESTER
Anton Mosimann

Ingredients

8 whole red mullet, each weighing about
   5oz / 145g
salt & freshly ground pepper

Vinaigrette sauce
2 fl oz / 60ml red wine vinegar
4 fl oz / 120ml olive oil
1/5 oz / 5g finely chopped shallot
a little chopped parsley & basil

Garnish
1oz / 30g blanched, tunelled & sliced carrot
1oz / 30g blanched, finely chopped onion
8 small basil leaves

Method

Gut the red mullet, wash thoroughly &
fillet carefully.

Cut 3 notches on the skin side of each
fillet, season & steam for 3-4 minutes.

For the sauce, mix together thoroughly
the vinegar, oil & shallot, then add the
herbs & season to taste.

Arrange the steamed fillets under a
cloche, skin side upwards, & garnish with
the blanched vegetables & basil leaves.

This can be served as a first course, in
which case halve the quantities; and of
course it can be served without the cloche.

Fillet of beef with rosemary & mustard

THE DORCHESTER
Anton Mosimann

Ingredients

4 fillet steaks, each weighing 5oz / 145g
2/3 oz / 20g finely chopped shallot
1 tsp finely chopped garlic
14 fl oz / 420 ml brown veal stock (see page 150)
3 oz / 85g fresh breadcrumbs
2 tsp freshly chopped parsley
2 tsp freshly chopped rosemary
juice of 1/2 lemon
2 tsp English mustard
salt & freshly ground pepper

Method

Trim the steaks of any fat & season with salt & pepper.

Sauté in a hot non-stick pan for about 2 minutes each side, remove from the pan & keep warm.

Add the shallot & garlic to the pan & sauté at a lower temperature, stirring constantly, until transparent.

Add the stock & boil rapidly until reduced by half.

Meanwhile, mix together the breadcrumbs & herbs, then add the lemon juice.

Brush one side of the steaks with the mustard, top with the herb mixture & place under a hot grill for 1-2 minutes until golden-brown.

Pour the well-seasoned sauce on to 4 plates, lay one steak on each & garnish with vegetables of your choice.

Scallop mousse with Beurre Blanc

DOYLE'S
Stella Doyle

Ingredients

6oz / 170g scallops
1 egg
4 fl oz / 120 ml whipping cream
softened butter
salt, pepper & nutmeg

Sauce

5 fl oz / 150 ml dry white wine
4 black peppercorns
1 sprig parsley
½ bay leaf
2 fl oz / 60ml whipping cream
4oz / 115g butter

Method

Ensure all ingredients are chilled.

Put the scallops into a processor with salt, pepper & nutmeg.

Process briefly, then add the egg, blend, then gradually add the cream.

Butter 4 dariole moulds, fill with the mousse, then place in a bain-marie.

Cook in an oven preheated to 350°F/ 180°C/gas 4 for 15-20 minutes.

For the sauce, put the wine, peppercorns & herbs into a saucepan & reduce to about 1 tbsp liquid.

Add the cream, boil, then add butter.

Stir until the butter is dissowed, strain & season to taste.

To serve, pour a little sauce on to 4 warmed plates, unmould one mousse on to each & garnish as desired. Serve immediately.

Salmon baked en papillotes

Ingredients

4 oz / 115g butter
4 oz / 115g finely diced carrot
4 oz / 115g finely diced red pepper
2 oz / 60g finely chopped onion
4 salmon steaks, each 6 oz / 170g
salt & pepper

Method

Melt 2 oz / 60g butter in a small pan & add the carrot, red pepper & onion; season & cook gently until slightly softened, then remove from heat & allow to cool.

Cut 4 heart-shaped pieces of greaseproof paper large enough to wrap around each salmon steak.

Lay the papers flat on a table, brush with a little melted butter & lay a salmon steak on the centre of each.

Season, cover with the vegetables, top with the remaining butter & close the paper tightly around the fish.

Place the parcels on a baking tray & cook in an oven preheated to 400°F / 200°C / gas 6 for about 10 minutes.

Remove from the oven & serve immediately in the paper bags, so that as each bag is punctured, the delicious aroma escapes.

Pheasant with winter vegetables & pine kernels

DUNDERRY LODGE
Catherine Healy

Ingredients

1 oz / 30g pine kernels
1 oz / 30g butter
1 oz / 30g chopped shallot
2 pheasant livers
1 fl oz / 30 ml sweet Madeira
6 rosemary leaves
1 tbsp breadcrumbs
4 pheasant breasts
4 tbsp shredded & blanched root vegetables.
   eg. celeriac, turnip, parsnip, celery &
   carrot
2 fl oz / 60 ml dry Dubonnet, Noilly Prat or
   Tio Pepe
7 fl oz / 210 ml double cream
1 oz / 30g butter
salt & pepper

Method

Pound the pine kernels in a mortar.

Melt the butter in a small pan, add the shallot & livers & cook quickly for a few minutes.

Add the Madeira & rosemary & cook for a further minute.

Allow to cool slightly & blend roughly in a food processor.

Add the breadcrumbs, pine kernels & seasoning & mix together to form a stiff paste.

Make a deep incision in the side of each pheasant breast & fill with one-quarter of the liver mixture.

Cut 4 squares of aluminium foil measuring 6"/15 cm, place one-quarter of the vegetables mixture in the centre of each, set a pheasant breast on top, season lightly & sprinkle with the dry Dubonnet, Noilly Prat or Tio Pepe.

Wrap up each parcel & bake in an oven preheated to 375°F/190°C/gas 5 for 30 minutes.

Open the foil parcels carefully, pour off the cooking juices into a small saucepan & add the cream.

Arrange the pheasant & vegetables on a serving dish & keep warm.

Reduce the sauce until slightly thickened, whisk in the butter & season to taste.

Pour over the pheasant & serve at once.

Gratin of potatoes & Jerusalem artichokes

DUNDERRY LODGE
Catherine Healy

Ingredients

1½ lb / 680g potatoes
8 oz / 225g Jerusalem artichokes
½ clove garlic (optional)
13 fl oz / 400 ml double cream
salt & pepper

Method

Peel & thinly slice the potatoes & artichokes.

Season with salt & pepper & arrange in layers in a buttered gratin dish which has been rubbed with the cut clove of garlic, if desired.

Pour over the cream & bake in an oven preheated to 375°F / 190°C / gas 5 for 1¼ hours.

Press the potatoes flat during cooking so that a crisp, even, golden-brown colour is achieved.

Winter Salad

<u>Ingredients</u>

1½ fl oz / 50ml virgin olive oil
1 tsp balsamic vinegar or good wine
   vinegar
1 head raddichio
6 heads mâche (lamb's lettuce)
½ cup rocket
½ cup winter purslane
1 dessp roasted sunflower seeds
salt & pepper

<u>Method</u>

Mix the oil & vinegar with the salt &
pepper.
Wash & carefully dry all the salad
leaves, toss in a large bowl with the
dressing, sprinkle with the sunflower seeds
& serve.

Lavender & honey ice-cream

<u>Ingredients</u>

½ tbsp dried lavender
1 tbsp boiling water
1 tbsp honey
10 fl oz / 300ml double cream
10 fl oz / 300ml fresh custard (see page 155)

<u>Method</u>

Infuse the lavender in the boiling water
for 10 minutes.
Strain carefully while still hot into the
honey, then mix together.
Add to the cream & custard & either churn
in an ice-cream maker according to the
manufacturer's instructions, or place in a
domestic freezer, beating at regular
intervals to prevent the formation of ice
crystals.
Serve in scoops, garnished with
crystallised violets.

Marinaded fresh salmon & scallops

FISCHER'S
Max Fischer

Ingredients

7oz / 200g fresh salmon
8 fresh scallops
2oz / 60g celery, cut into thin matchsticks
2oz / 60g cucumber, cut into thin matchsticks
2oz / 60g finely chopped shallot
juice of ½ lemon
juice of ½ lime
salt & freshly ground white pepper
1½ fl oz / 45ml olive oil
finely chopped chervil, dill & coriander

Method

Slice the salmon & scallops very thinly.
Arrange the fish attractively on 4 plates.
Sprinkle the remaining ingredients over the fish in the order given, & leave to marinade for about 10 minutes before serving.

Sea bass in a tomato & ginger sauce

Ingredients

FISCHER'S

4 fillets sea bass, each 6oz / 170g
1/3oz / 10g coriander seeds
1oz / 30g finely chopped shallot
4 sprigs thyme
salt & freshly ground white pepper

Sauce

8oz / 225g tomatoes
1oz / 30g butter
2oz / 60g finely chopped onion
1 bay leaf
1 sprig thyme
2oz / 60g finely chopped shallot
1 small piece fresh root ginger, peeled & cut into fine matchsticks
7 fl oz / 210ml white wine
7 fl oz / 210ml double cream
2oz / 60g butter

Method

Sprinkle the sea bass with the coriander seeds, shallot, thyme, salt & white pepper, then steam for about 5 minutes — it should retain a slight translucence in the centre.

For the sauce, put the tomatoes into boiling water for 10 seconds, remove, skin & cut in half horizontally.

Remove the seeds & chop the flesh finely.

Melt the butter in a pan, add the onion, soften, then add the tomato dice & cook until reduced to a purée.

Add the bay leaf, thyme, shallot, ginger & wine, bring to the boil & reduce by one-third.

Remove the bay leaf & thyme, add the cream & reduce further to a smooth consistency.

Add the 2oz / 60g butter & stir until melted.

Pour the sauce on to plates & place the sea bass on top of the sauce.

Serve immediately

43

Délices aux poires

Ingredients

Max Fischer
Fischer's

Pears
1½ pt / 1 ltr water
2¼ lb / 1 kg sugar
½ stick cinnamon
½ vanilla pod
2 whole cloves
peel from 1 lemon
10 medium-sized pears

Pear mousse
3 leaves gelatine (or an 11g packet of powdered gelatine)
2 egg yolks
2 oz / 60g castor sugar
2 fl oz / 60 ml eau-de-vie de poire william
8 fl oz / 240 ml pear purée (see method)
5 fl oz / 150 ml double cream

Pear sorbet
6 fl oz / 200 ml pear purée (see method)
3 fl oz / 100 ml pear syrup
3 fl oz / 100 ml medium white wine
2 fl oz / 60 ml eau-de-vie de poire william
juice of 1 lemon

Passion-fruit sorbet
6 fl oz / 200 ml passion-fruit juice
3 fl oz / 100 ml stock syrup
3 fl oz / 100 ml medium white wine

Chocolate sabayon
4 egg yolks
1½ oz / 45g castor sugar
1 tbsp cocoa powder
4 fl oz / 125 ml milk
1 fl oz / 45 ml crème de cacao

44

Method

For the pears, put the first 6 ingredients into a saucepan & bring to the boil.

Simmer gently for 30 minutes & strain.

Peel the pears. leaving the stalk intact, & use a potato peeler or scoop to remove most of the core from the base.

Place immediately in the hot syrup, cover with greaseproof paper & poach very gently until tender but firm.

Select the 4 best pears & set aside, & purée the remainder in a processor.

For the pear mousse, soften the leaf gelatine in cold water, or dissolve the powdered gelatine in a little hot water.

Whisk the egg yolks & sugar in a basin & add the eau-de-vie.

Warm a little of the pear purée & blend the gelatine in it.

Add to the yolks with the remaining purée & set aside until it becomes firm.

Whip the double cream until thick & fold into the mixture. Refrigerate for at least an hour.

For the pear sorbet, combine all the ingredients & freeze in an ice-cream maker or in a tray in the deep freeze. If using the latter method, remove each half-hour during freezing & whisk.

For the passion-fruit sorbet, combine all the ingredients & freeze as for the pear sorbet.

For the chocolate sabayon, put all the ingredients in a basin & whisk over hot water until the mixture doubles in quantity & thickens.

To serve, place a whole drained pear in the centre of a large plate.

Using a dessertspoon dipped in hot water, put a scoop of each sorbet & one of pear mousse around the pear.

Pour a little warm chocolate sabayon over the pear & serve immediately.

Soufflé suissesse

LE GAVROCHE
Albert Roux

Ingredients

5 oz / 145g butter
2 oz / 60g flour
28 fl oz / 700 ml milk
5 egg yolks
1 tbsp butter cut into small pieces
35 fl oz / 1 ltr double cream
6 egg whites
8 oz / 225g grated Gruyère or Emmental cheese
salt & freshly ground white pepper

Method

Melt 2 oz / 60g butter in a small pan over low heat; stir in the flour using a small wire whisk & cook gently for 2 or 3 minutes, stirring continuously.

Take the pan off the heat & leave the roux to cool slightly.

Bring the milk to the boil & pour over the cooled roux, whisking all the time; set the pan over high heat, bring the mixture to the boil, stirring continuously, & cook for 3 minutes.

Take off the heat, stir in the egg yolks, season to taste, dot with 1 tbsp butter to prevent a skin forming & set aside at room temperature.

Meanwhile, chill 8 round 3"/8cm tartlet tins by putting them in the freezer for a few minutes; after removing, immediately butter them generously & set on a baking sheet.

Pour the cream into a gratin dish, add a little salt & warm gently without boiling.

Beat the egg whites with a pinch of salt until they form stiff peaks.

Pour the soufflé mixture into a wide-rimmed bowl &, using a whisk, quickly beat in about one-third of the egg whites.

Carefully fold in the remainder with a spatula, then, using a tablespoon, heap up the mixture in the tartlet tins to form 8 large mounds.

Bake the soufflés in an oven preheated to 400°F/200°C/gas 6 for 3 minutes, until the tops become golden.

Remove from the oven &, protecting your hands with a cloth, turn out each soufflé into the dish of warm cream.

Sprinkle with the cheese & return to the oven for 5 minutes.

Serve immediately using a spoon & fork, taking care not to crush the soufflés.

Note: This is an original way of serving a cheese soufflé. The cheese is not incorporated into the soufflé mixture but is used to glaze it. As it cooks, the soufflé absorbs the cream and will be very rich & creamy. Nevertheless it is a light dish with a wonderful aroma, which has delighted diners at Le Gavroche since the day the restaurant opened.

Sablé aux fraises

LE GAVROCHE
Albert Roux

Ingredients

Shortbread
5oz / 145g butter
4 oz / 115g sifted icing sugar
pinch salt
1 egg
9 oz / 250g sifted plain flour
1 drop vanilla or lemon essence
1 oz / 30g ground almonds
1 egg yolk beaten with 1 tbsp milk for glaze

Coulis
2½oz / 75g sugar
4 fl oz / 120 ml water
½ oz / 15g glucose
9 oz / 250g red soft fruits
juice of ½ lemon

Fruit
1 lb 12 oz / 800g strawberries, raspberries or
   wild strawberries (reserve 4 for garnish)

Method

For the shortbread, cut the butter into small pieces, place on a cool surface, work with the fingertips until very soft, add the icing sugar & salt & blend thoroughly.

Break in the egg, mix lightly, add the flour, essence & ground almonds &, still using the fingers, amalgamate thoroughly.

Shape the pastry into a ball, wrap in greaseproof paper or polythene & refrigerate for several hours.

When ready, roll out on a lightly floured surface to a thickness of 1/16" / 2 mm; cut 12 plain circles of 4" / 10 cm diameter, place on a baking sheet & glaze 4 of them.

Bake in an oven preheated to 400°F / 200°C / gas 6 for 8 minutes, remove, cool slightly, transfer to a wire rack with a palette knife & cool completely.

For the coulis, place the sugar, water & glucose in a heavy-based pan, set over high heat & bring to the boil, stirring occasionally with a wooden spatula.

Boil for several minutes, skimming the surface as necessary, then pass through a conical sieve & leave to cool.

Hull, wash & drain the fruit, purée in a processor or blender with the syrup & lemon juice, rub through a conical sieve & refrigerate until required.

For the fruit, wash & hull, halve if large, roll in two-thirds of the coulis & refrigerate until required.

To serve, place an unglazed shortbread base on each of 4 plates, spread with some of the fruit, place a second shortbread circle on top, add another layer of fruit & finish with a glazed shortbread circle topped with a whole strawberry or raspberry.

Serve the remainder of the coulis separately.

Note: do not assemble this dish until just before serving, as the coulis will cause the shortbread to soften.

Chocolate fudge cake

Shaun Hill & Kay Henderson
Gidleigh Park

Ingredients

8 oz / 225g dark chocolate
8 oz / 225g soft butter
8 oz / 225g castor sugar
6 eggs, separated
few drops vanilla essence
4 oz / 115g ground almonds
5 oz / 145g fresh breadcrumbs

Icing

4 oz / 115g castor sugar
3 oz / 85g butter
6 oz / 170g icing sugar
2 oz / 60g cocoa powder
4 tbsp water

Method

Melt the chocolate in a basin standing over hot water.

Cream the butter & sugar until light in colour, add the egg yolks & vanilla essence & beat well.

Add the ground almonds, mix in, then fold in the melted chocolate & breadcrumbs.

Beat the egg whites until stiff but not dry, & fold gently into the mixture.

Pour into a buttered 7"/17cm cake tin & bake for approximately 60 minutes in an oven preheated to 350°F/180°C/gas 4.

A skewer inserted into the centre of the cake should come out clean when the cake is cooked.

Remove the cake from the tin & allow to go cold.

For the icing, melt the castor sugar & butter in a saucepan.

Sieve the icing sugar & cocoa into a bowl, add the butter & sugar mixture & the water.

Mix well until smooth & allow to cool.

When the icing begins to harden & set, spread quickly over the top & sides of the cake.

North Sea fish soup

Ingredients

GIDLEIGH PARK

8 oz / 225g scallops
3 oz / 85g haddock fillets
3 oz / 85g sea bass fillets
3 oz / 85g hake fillets
3 oz / 85g shelled whole prawns (keep shells)
juice of 1/2 lemon
1 pt / 500ml fish stock (see page 151 & method below)
4 parsley stalks
2 oz / 60g chopped shallot
2 egg yolks
2 fl oz / 60ml double cream
1 skinned, seeded & chopped large tomato
1 tbsp chopped parsley
salt & cayenne pepper

Method

Cut the fish into fairly large pieces according to texture (e.g. turbot smaller than scallop) so that it will all cook in the same time, mix with the lemon juice & season.

Make a well-flavoured stock using the fish bones, prawn shells & parsley stalks (see page 151).

Bring the stock to the boil, add the fish & shallots, bring to the boil again, then remove from the heat.

Mix the egg yolks & cream together in a basin, pour a little of the soup into this mixture, stirring continuously, then add the liaison to the soup without reboiling.

Add the tomato & parsley & serve at once.

This soup is delicious only when made with very fresh fish. Resist the temptation to put too much cream in it. Finally, make it at the last minute so that the fish does not dry out & overcook.

Venison noisettes with marc de Bourgogne

Ingredients

2 lb / 900g boned saddle of venison (ask the
  butcher for the bones)
8 oz / 225g diced mixed leek, carrot, onion &
  celery
5 fl oz / 150ml game or veal stock (see page 150)
3 oz / 85g unsalted butter
1 fl oz / 30ml Sauternes
2 fl oz / 60ml marc de Bourgogne
1 oz / 30g butter
a little oil
salt & pepper
To serve
fresh seasonal vegetables

Method

  Cut the saddle into slices & reserve.
  Colour the bones & vegetables in a frying
pan, add the stock, simmer for half an
hour, strain, then reduce by half.
  Whisk in the unsalted butter until the
sauce thickens, add the Sauternes & marc de
Bourgogne, & keep hot.
  Season the venison noisettes & cook in
butter & oil in a frying pan.
  Serve the noisettes coated with the sauce
& garnished with fresh seasonal vegetables.

Hambleton's rice pudding with exotic fruits

HAMBLETON HALL
Brian Baker

<u>Ingredients</u>

15 fl oz / 450 ml milk
¼ vanilla pod or ½ tsp vanilla essence
½ oz / 15g butter
1½ oz / 45g castor sugar
2 oz / 60g short-grain rice
5 fl oz / 150 ml double cream
1 whole egg
2 egg yolks
selection of exotic fruits, e.g. mangoes,
  pawpaws, passion fruit, lychees, guavas,
  pineapple & oranges
juice of 2 oranges
juice of 2 passion fruit

Method

In a heavy casserole bring 12 fl oz /360 ml of the milk to the boil with the vanilla pod or essence, removing the pod, if used, when boiling point is reached.

Add the butter & sugar & stir gently until the sugar is dissolved; allow to cool slightly, then pour in the rice.

Bring to the boil, cover & cook in an oven preheated to 325°F/170°C/ gas 3 for 30 minutes, without stirring.

Remove from the oven & cool slightly.

Whisk together the remaining milk, the cream, egg & egg yolks & add to the cooled pudding, using a little more sugar at this stage if required.

Spoon the pudding into individual buttered moulds (or one large one) & cook in the oven at the same temperature, but this time in a bain-marie, for a further 30-40 minutes, until set.

Remove from the oven & cool.

Prepare the chosen fruits, either slicing them or cutting them into small cubes.

Mix the orange & passion-fruit juices together & pour over the prepared fruits.

When the rice is cold, unmould & serve surrounded by the fruits.

Rutland Water trout wrapped in puff pastry with a Bramley & cider sauce HAMBLETON HALL

Ingredients

1 pink - fleshed trout of about 2 lb / 900g
1 lb / 450g puff pastry (see page 152)
1 egg for egg wash
salt & cayenne pepper

Mousseline

1 trout of about 8oz / 225g
1 egg white
5 fl oz / 150 ml double cream
4 oz / 115g peeled, cored & finely diced
   apples (preferably Bramley)
2oz / 60g diced button mushrooms
1 tbsp chopped chives

Sauce

2oz / 60g chopped shallot
4oz / 115g mushroom stalks
1 tbsp chopped chervil
2oz / 60g fresh fennel stalks
4oz / 115g white fish trimmings
6oz / 170g peeled, cored & diced apples
10 fl oz / 300 ml dry cider
1pt / 500ml fish stock
8 fl oz / 240 ml double cream
juice of 1 lemon
3 oz / 85g unsalted butter in cubes

Garnish

2oz / 60g peeled, cored & finely diced
   apples
few sprigs chervil

Method

Ask the fishmonger to clean & fillet both trout, then wash them & remove any bones.

For the mousseline, skin the smaller fillets & purée them in a food processor with the egg white, gradually beat in the double cream, add the diced apples, mushrooms & chives, then season to taste.

To assemble, take a large fillet, skin side down, spread with the mousseline, then top with the second fillet, skin side up.

Roll out the puff pastry to an even thickness of 1/16"/2mm, & lay the fish gently on half of it, damp the edges of the pastry, fold over to enclose the fish & press the edges together.

Trim the pastry to the shape of the fish, egg-wash, then mark on scales, gills & an eye using an icing nozzle.

Place in the refrigerator for at least 20 minutes, then bake in an oven preheated to 400°F/200°C/gas 6 for about 35 minutes, or until the pastry is golden.

For the sauce, place the shallot, mushroom stalks, chervil, fennel, fish trimmings, apples, cider & fish stock in a heavy-based pan, bring to the boil & simmer until reduced by half.

Add the cream & simmer until the liquid has thickened & reduced to a coating consistency.

Remove from the heat, pass through a fine sieve into a clean pan, return to the heat & bring back to a simmer, then adjust seasoning with salt, pepper & lemon juice.

Whisk in the unsalted butter, then finally garnish with the small apple dice.

To serve, place the cooked trout on a serving dish, pour the cider sauce around & garnish with small bunches of chervil.

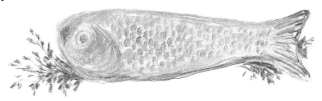

A little idea from Japan with beef & ginger

HINTLESHAM HALL
Robert Mabey

Ingredients

a little oil
8oz / 225g beef fillet (tail end)
a bowl of iced water

Dipping sauce

½" / 1cm piece peeled & finely chopped fresh ginger
½ peeled & finely chopped clove garlic

1 small peeled & finely chopped shallot
juice of 1/2 lemon
1 fl oz / 30 ml light soy sauce
2 fl oz / 60 ml sesame oil
3 fl oz / 90 ml vegetable oil

Sauce garnish

1 very finely dried small carrot
1/2 very finely dried stalk celery
3 very finely dried spring onions
5 chopped small heads parsley

Presentation garnish

1 leek cut into very fine strips, held in
    iced water
2 tsp toasted sesame seeds

Method

Heat a little oil in a pan until very hot
& smoking, then quickly sear the beef
fillet.
   When well sealed, plunge into iced water,
allow to cool, remove & drain well.
   For the dipping sauce, place all the
ingredients except the oils in a liquidiser
or processor & blend well.
   Slowly add the oils until an emulsion is
formed.
   Stir in the sauce garnish.
   Presentation: slice the beef very finely,
arrange on a small bed of drained leek
strips & sprinkle with sesame seeds.
   Serve the dipping sauce in 4 small bowls.
Each person takes a piece of beef &
garnish, & dips this into the sauce.
   The dish should be served ice-cold.
   Serves 4 as a starter.

Roast bananas with pancakes & vanilla ice-cream, perfumed with maple caramel

HINTLESHAM HALL

Ingredients

Ice-cream
1 pt / 500 ml milk
1 vanilla pod or a few drops vanilla essence
6 egg yolks
4 oz / 115 g sugar

Pancakes
10 fl oz / 300 ml milk
1 egg
½ oz / 15 g sugar
4 oz / 115 g sieved plain flour
½ oz / 15 g melted butter

Sauce
4 oz / 115 g sugar
1 fl oz / 30 ml water
4 fl oz / 120 ml maple syrup

To complete
1 oz / 30 g unsalted butter
4 large bananas, not too ripe

Method

For the ice-cream, boil the milk with the vanilla, then remove the pod, if used.

Beat the eggs & sugar together & pour the hot milk on top, whisking all the time.

Return to the pan & cook over a low heat, stirring continuously with a wooden spoon until the custard reaches a coating consistency.

Pour through a sieve into a clean bowl.

If you have an ice-cream machine, churn according to the maker's instructions; if not, place the ice-cream in the freezer & whisk every 15 minutes until frozen to prevent the formation of ice crystals.

For the pancakes, mix a little milk with the egg & sugar & slowly whisk in the sieved flour to form a stiff paste.

Beat well to remove any lumps, then add the rest of the liquid, beating all the time, & finally the melted butter.

Cook the pancakes as thinly as possible - you should be able to make 12 in a 6"/15cm pan.

Fold each pancake in 4 & keep warm.

For the sauce, melt the sugar in the water & cook until it is the colour of caramel.

Plunge the base of the pan into cold water to stop further cooking, then add the maple syrup.

To complete, heat the butter in a frying pan until it starts to bubble, add the peeled bananas & allow to brown.

When done, transfer to an oven preheated to 350°F/180°C/gas 4 for 5 to 10 minutes, or until the bananas are soft.

Meanwhile, heat half the sauce in a shallow pan, add the pancakes & warm through, turning once.

To serve, arrange the bananas & pancakes on 4 heated plates & pour over the remainder of the sauce.

Serve immediately with the ice-cream.

61

Stuffed duckling with lentils in cream and garlic

HOMEWOOD PARK
Stephen Ross

Ingredients

2 small fresh ducklings
salt & pepper

Stuffing
1 oz / 30g butter
2 oz / 60g finely chopped onion
4 oz / 115g finely chopped mushrooms
zest & juice of 1 orange
chopped leaves of 1 sprig thyme
chopped leaves of 2 sprigs basil
1 egg
4 oz / 115g (approx) fresh brown breadcrumbs

Sauce
8 oz / 225g mixed lentils
1½ oz / 45g diced bacon
1 clove garlic
10 fl oz / 300 ml stock (see page 148)
5 fl oz / 150 ml double cream

Method

Remove the legs & breasts from the ducks.
Trim the sinews from the breasts and bone out the legs by scraping meat down from the thigh end to the drumstick, chopping off just past the knuckle. This will leave small pockets where the bones have been removed.

For the stuffing, melt the butter in a saucepan, add the finely chopped onion & cook until soft.

Add the mushrooms, orange zest & juice, & herbs, cook for a few minutes & remove from the heat.

When cool, beat in the egg, season with

62

salt & pepper & add enough breadcrumbs to make a smooth stuffing.

Put the stuffing into the legs & secure the top with cocktail sticks or string.

For the sauce, soak the lentils in cold water overnight, then drain & rinse.

Fry the bacon & garlic in a little oil, add the stock & lentils, & cook until soft – about 15-20 minutes.

To cook the duck, put the legs into a roasting tray, brush with oil & season with salt & pepper.

Cook in an oven preheated to 375°F/190°C/gas 5 for about 45 minutes.

Season the duck breasts with salt & pepper & put into hot oil in a frying pan, keeping them flesh side down for a minute to seal before turning them over.

Finish cooking them in the oven for 5 minutes, remove, cover with a lid & keep warm for 10 minutes to allow the meat to set properly.

When the lentils are cooked, add the double cream, reheat, & season to taste.

To serve, put the sauce on to plates, remove the cocktail sticks or string from the duck legs & place them on top of the sauce.

Remove the skin from the breasts, if desired, slice them & arrange on top of the sauce.

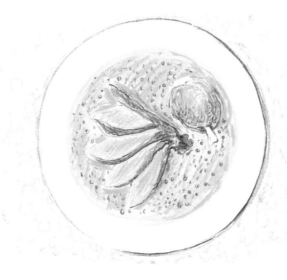

Smoked breasts of quail with mange-tout peas & a truffle & herb sauce

HUNSTRETE HOUSE
Robert Elsmore

Ingredients

8 oz / 225g mange-tout peas
a little walnut oil
1 golden purslane lettuce
1 red lollo lettuce
4 skinned, smoked quail breasts

Sauce

1/2 fresh truffle
2 tbsp truffle liquor
2 tbsp Dijon mustard
1 fl oz / 30ml Madeira
1 fl oz / 30ml port
1/2 fl oz / 15ml sherry vinegar
1/2 fl oz / 15ml white wine vinegar
4 fl oz / 120ml walnut oil
4 fl oz / 120ml vegetable oil
4 fl oz / 120ml olive oil
1 fl oz / 30ml double cream
1 tsp each chopped fresh parsley, basil,
    chives & dill
1/4 tsp chopped fresh mint
salt & pepper

Method

   For the sauce, liquidise the first 7 sauce ingredients for about one minute in a food processor or blender.
   Add the remaining sauce ingredients & process for 2 more minutes.
   Adjust the seasoning to taste & sharpen with a little more mustard, if desired.
   Top & tail the mange-tout peas, blanch briefly in boiling water & refresh in cold.
   Slice diagonally, season, toss in a little walnut oil, then arrange in a ring on 4 plates.
   Wash the lettuces, pat dry & tear into bite-sized pieces; toss in a little walnut oil & arrange in the centre of the mange-tout circle.
   Slice the quail breasts diagonally, place on top of the lettuce & brush lightly with oil.
   Pour the sauce around & serve at once.

Delicate ragoût of chicken & mussels in basil & Pernod sauce

Paul Gayler
INIGO JONES

Ingredients

1½ oz / 45g butter
2 oz / 60g roughly chopped shallot
a few parsley stalks
2 pt / 1 ltr mussels
2 fl oz / 60ml white wine
2 pt / 1 ltr chicken stock
  (see page 148)
a little olive oil
1 sliced & diced medium leek
2 sliced & diced medium carrots
1 sliced & diced stick celery
1 sliced & diced piece fennel
½ crushed clove garlic
1 sprig thyme
1 bayleaf
3 firm tomatoes, blanched, seeded & cut
  into small dice
4 chicken breasts, each 6 oz / 170g
2 fl oz / 60ml Pernod
4 fl oz / 120 ml double cream
pinch saffron powder
salt & pepper

Garnish
chopped fresh basil & chives.

Method

Butter a pan, place in it the shallot, parsley stalks & scrubbed mussels, moisten with the wine & add half of the chicken stock.

Cover with a lid, & steam the mussels until the shells open – about 1 minute.

Pour the mussels into a colander & cool.

Take the mussels from their shells, remove the beards, & strain the cooking liquor to remove any sand.

Place the remaining 1oz / 30g butter and oil in another pan, add the vegetables, garlic, thyme, bay leaf & tomatoes, & cook gently for 2-3 minutes.

Place the seasoned chicken breasts on top, moisten with Pernod, add the mussel stock & the remaining chicken stock, cover with buttered paper & poach gently until cooked.

Remove the chicken breasts & keep warm.

Reduce the cooking liquor & finish with the cream & saffron.

Add the cleaned mussels to the sauce, reheat, check seasoning & add the herbs.

To serve, cut the chicken into small escalopes, pour the sauce over & serve immediately.

Fillet of pork with spinach, wild mushrooms & port wine sauce

INIGO JONES
Paul Gayler

Ingredients

2 large pork fillets
2oz / 60g wild mushrooms (girolles, pieds de mouton, pleurottes, paris)
3oz / 80g spinach
2oz / 60g chopped shallot
2oz / 60g butter
1 fl oz / 30 ml oil
2 fl oz / 60 ml double cream
4oz / 115g pig caul (crépinettes)
1 sprig rosemary
3 fl oz / 90 ml port wine
4 fl oz / 120 ml veal stock (see page 151)
Salt, pepper & nutmeg

Garnish

16 asparagus tips (optional)
chervil

Method

Prepare the pork fillets: trim well & remove any sinews.

Clean & prepare the mushrooms, cutting them into ½"/1 cm dice.

Pick over the spinach & wash well, blanch in boiling water for 30 seconds, refresh in cold water, squeeze out excess water & dry in a cloth.

In a saucepan soften half the shallot in a little butter, add the mushrooms & sauté.

Lightly chop the spinach, add to the mushrooms, cook gently until dry, then add a little double cream to bind the mixture lightly.

Season to taste & allow to cool.

Cut the pork fillets into 8 medallions, each approximately 2 oz / 60g in weight, season, seal in a hot frying pan, remove & cool.

Place a spoonful of the mushroom & spinach mixture on top of each medallion.

Wrap each one in a piece of pig's caul, then cook briefly in oil in a hot pan to seal.

Transfer to an oven preheated to 375°F/190°C/gas 5 for about 10 minutes.

When cooked remove from the oven, drain & keep warm.

Add to the cooking pan the remaining chopped shallot, the rosemary, port & veal stock.

Reduce to a coating consistency, finish with a little butter, then strain.

To serve, place 2 medallions on each plate, garnish with a criss-cross pattern of asparagus tips (if used), pour sauce around the pork & decorate with chervil.

Turban of smoked Mallaig haddock with queen scallops & champagne sauce

INVERLOCHY CASTLE
Graham Newbould

Ingredients

Haddock Mousse
4 oz / 115 g skinned lemon sole fillets
4 oz / 115 g scallops
4 oz / 115 g skinned smoked haddock fillets
1 egg white
10 fl oz / 300 ml double cream

Haddock filling
1 oz / 30 g butter
1 oz / 30 g flour
10 fl oz / 300 ml milk
12 oz / 340 g skinned smoked haddock fillets

Champagne sauce
bones from 3 Dover soles
10 fl oz / 300 ml dry white wine
1 pt / 500 ml fish stock (see page 151)
2 oz / 60 g sliced shallot
1 oz / 30 g sliced button mushrooms
pinch sugar
10 fl oz / 300 ml double cream
6 fl oz / 170 ml champagne

Garnish
16 queen scallops / 4 regular scallops
a little dry white wine
few sprigs chervil
salt & cayenne pepper

Method

For the mousse, blend the sole, scallops & smoked haddock in a food processor with the egg white, then gradually beat in the double cream & season with salt & cayenne.

Carefully spoon the mousse into one large or 4 individual buttered turban moulds, then cover with buttered greaseproof paper & aluminium foil.

Cook in a bain-marie in an oven preheated to 350°F / 180°C / gas 4 for 10-15 minutes, until firm to the touch.

For the haddock filling, melt the butter in a saucepan, stir in the flour & cook gently for a few minutes.

Gradually add the cold milk, stirring continuously until it is all incorporated, bring to the boil & simmer for 30 minutes.

Meanwhile, poach the haddock in either milk or water until cooked, then drain & flake the fish into the sauce.

For the champagne sauce, put the sole bones, wine, fish stock, shallot, mushrooms & sugar into a saucepan, bring to the boil & reduce until there is only about 5 fl oz/ 150 ml liquid remaining.

Add the cream, boil & reduce by one-third.

Boil the champagne in another saucepan until reduced by half, add to the sauce. Strain through a fine sieve, season to taste & keep hot.

For the garnish, poach the scallops briefly in a little white wine, then return them to their shells.

To serve, turn out the haddock mousse on to a plate & pour the haddock filling into the centre.

Coat lightly with the champagne sauce & garnish with the scallops & some sprigs of chervil.

71

Fig & hazelnut strudel with Grand Marnier butter sauce

INVERLOCHY CASTLE
Graham Newbould

Ingredients

8 oz / 225g strudel pastry (see page 153) or
  4 sheets filo pastry
3 oz / 85g melted unsalted butter
4 oz / 115g ground almonds
finely grated zest of 1 lemon
4 oz / 115g soft brown sugar
1/3 oz / 10g ground cinnamon
7 oz / 200g toasted chopped hazelnuts
4 oz / 115g sultanas
12 fresh figs
a little icing sugar

Sauce
2 oz / 60g soft brown sugar
juice of 4 oranges
juice of 1/2 lemon
finely grated zest of 2 oranges
3 fl oz / 90ml Grand Marnier
4 oz / 115g unsalted butter

Method

Roll out the strudel pastry very thinly on a floured cloth, allow to rest for 15 minutes, then brush with melted butter.

If using filo, lay 2 sheets on a dry cloth, slightly overlapping along one edge, brush with melted butter, lay the remaining 2 sheets on top, overlapping in the same way, & brush again with melted butter.

Sprinkle the ground almonds & lemon zest over two-thirds of the pastry.

Mix together the sugar, cinnamon, chopped hazelnuts & sultanas & sprinkle over the almonds.

Peel & slice the figs & lay these on top of the other ingredients.

Using the cloth, carefully roll the pastry over the ingredients as if making a Swiss roll, keeping the end at the underside to seal the roll.

Place on a greased baking sheet & brush well with melted butter.

Bake in an oven preheated to 400°F /200°C/ gas 6 for 15 minutes, remove, brush with melted butter & return to bake for a further 10-15 minutes.

When the strudel is cooked, remove from the oven & dust with icing sugar.

Meanwhile, for the sauce, place all the ingredients except the butter in a saucepan, bring to the boil & simmer until reduced by half.

Gradually whisk in the butter to make a smooth sauce.

To serve, slice the strudel & arrange on 4 plates; hand the sauce separately.

Kalamari ghemisto

KALAMARAS
Stelios Platanos

Ingredients

2 lb / 900g medium-sized squid
2 oz / 60g flour
2 fl oz / 60ml olive oil
4 chopped spring onions
1 crushed clove garlic
1 tbsp chopped parsley
4 sprigs chopped fresh mint
2 skinned, seeded & chopped tomatoes
2 fl oz / 60ml medium-dry white wine
4oz / 115g long-grain rice
salt & pepper

Method

Clean & prepare the squid: separate the head & tentacles together from the body, cut off the wings, remove the quill from the cavity, then separate the head from the tentacles by cutting just in front of the eyes.

Peel the purplish skin from the body & discard this, together with the head & quill.

Wash the squid pieces in cold water & dry well.

Season the sacs with salt, coat lightly in flour & fry in a little of the olive oil until golden-brown.

Chop the tentacles & wings into small pieces & fry in the remaining olive oil, together with the spring onion, garlic, parsley & mint.

Add the tomatoes & wine & cook for a few minutes, then add the rice, cover with cold water & simmer for 10 minutes.

Fill the sacs with the rice mixture, taking care not to overfill them as the rice will expand during final cooking.

Place the stuffed squid in a greased dish & bake in an oven preheated to 350°F/180°C/gas 4 for 35 minutes.

Serve hot with a mixed salad.

Winters in Greece can be hard. The sea gets very rough & there is a fierce wind in the hills. Housewives must prepare themselves against the severe weather, storing what they have from the last catch of fish before winter, & they are creative in making tasty dishes during the hard months. One such recipe is sacoula thalassini, which takes steamed or fried filleted fish (depending on the type of fish). A little olive oil is added, with wine, crushed garlic & sprigs of rosemary. The mixture is encased in filo pastry (sacoula, a small bag). Because of the preservative qualities of garlic & rosemary, the dish lasts for a few days.

Sacoula thalassini

KALAMARAS
Stelios Platanos

Ingredients

2 lb/900g boned fish fillets (choose any 2
  from red mullet, grey mullet, sea bass,
  salmon or halibut: you will need 8
  fillets in all); keep the bones
2 fl oz /60ml olive oil
4 roughly chopped spring onions
1 crushed clove garlic
small sprig fresh rosemary
1 diced carrot
1 diced leek
4 sprigs chopped fresh dill
4 fl oz / 120 ml dry white wine
8 sheets filo pastry
olive oil for brushing
salt & pepper

Method

Select 2 fish from the options given, perhaps either salmon or red mullet plus one of the others.

Trim the fish but leave the skin on so that they retain their shape during cooking.

Season the fillets & steam lightly, keeping them underdone.

Remove from the heat & allow to cool.

Heat 1 fl oz / 30 ml olive oil in a small saucepan & add the spring onions, garlic & rosemary.

Fry for a minute, then add the carrot, leek, dill, fish bones, wine & remaining olive oil.

Just cover with water, bring to the boil & continue boiling until only about 5 fl oz / 150 ml liquid remains, strain, allow to cool, then pour over the cooked fish fillets.

Lay 4 sheets of filo pastry on a clean surface & brush with olive oil.

Lay 4 more sheets on top of these & brush this second layer also with olive oil.

Place 2 fillets, 1 of each of the 2 fish, in the centre of each pastry portion & moisten with a little of the stock.

Bring the corners of each set of pastry sheets together & close securely to form a parcel or sack (saconta).

Place the parcels on a greased baking tray & cover the top of each with a small piece of foil to prevent the pastry burning.

Bake in an oven preheated to 400°F / 200°C / gas 6 for about 10-15 minutes, until the pastry is golden-brown.

Remove from the oven, discard the foil & serve immediately with either a green salad or some leaf spinach.

Soufflé aux épinards, sauce anchois

LANGAN'S BRASSERIE
Richard Shepherd

Ingredients

2½ oz / 75g butter
2½ oz / 75g flour
1 pt / 500 ml milk, heated with 1 onion,
   1 bay leaf & 1 clove
4 oz / 115g cooked chopped spinach
4 separated eggs
ground nutmeg, salt & cayenne pepper
Sauce
2 egg yolks
8 oz / 225g warm melted butter
squeeze lemon juice
1 small tin well-drained anchovy fillets

Method

Make a white sauce with the butter, flour
& milk & season with nutmeg, salt &
cayenne: add the egg yolks & spinach & mix
thoroughly.
   Beat the egg whites with a pinch of salt
until stiff, then fold into the spinach
mixture.
   Spoon into 6 well-buttered soufflé moulds
& bake in an oven preheated to 350°F / 180°C /
gas 4 for about 20 minutes.
   For the sauce, put the egg yolks in a
basin set over hot water, add 1 tbsp water &
cook gently, whisking continuously.
Cool slightly, slowly add the butter,
season to taste & add the lemon juice.
   Pound the anchovy fillets to a smooth
paste with a drop of water & whisk into the
sauce.
   Serve straight from the oven & hand the
sauce separately.
   Serves 6.

Spinach soufflé

Crème brûleé

<u>Ingredients</u>

1pt / 500ml double cream
3 egg yolks
4oz / 115g castor sugar
few drops vanilla essence
a little demerara sugar

<u>Method</u>

Bring three-quarters of the cream to the boil & remove from the heat.

Mix the rest of the cream, the egg yolks, castor sugar & vanilla essence together. Then add to the boiled cream.

Return to the heat, stirring constantly with a wooden spoon, & bring to just below boiling point.

Remove from the heat, divide between 4 ramekin dishes & allow to cool completely.

Sprinkle each ramekin with a little demerara sugar & glaze quickly under a hot grill.

Return to the refrigerator, allow to set, then serve.

Choc·o·block Stanley

McCOY'S
The McCoy brothers

Ingredients

5 oz / 145 g plain chocolate
7 egg yolks
8 oz / 225 g castor sugar
10 oz / 280 g softened unsalted butter
5 oz / 145 g cocoa powder
15 fl oz / 450 ml double cream
2 oz / 60 g icing sugar
14 sponge fingers (2 pkt boudoir biscuits)
4 fl oz / 120 ml cold, strong black coffee
1 pt / 500 ml fresh custard flavoured with
 1 dssp instant coffee powder (see page 155)

Method

Melt the chocolate in a basin over hot water; beat the egg yolks & castor sugar until light, then add to the chocolate.

Whisk the butter & cocoa powder until creamy & beat into the egg mixture.

Whisk the cream until it is of the same consistency as the chocolate mixture, whisk in the icing sugar, then add to the chocolate.

Brush the sponge fingers with the coffee & use them to line a rectangular or charlotte mould.

Fill with the chocolate mixture, then refrigerate for at least 3 hours.

To serve, coat plates with the coffee sauce & lay a slice of the choc-o-block on each.

Serves 12.

Stan from the cottage up the road was so impressed by the increasing flow of customers that he would say, when he came in for his pint, 'Choc-o-block tonight again?' So, when the McCoy brothers first made this pudding & it looked just like a block of chocolate, it was an obvious choice to call it 'Choc-o-block Stanley.'

80

Wild fungi in pastry

Ingredients

8 oz / 225g puff pastry (see page 152)
1 egg for egg wash
salt & pepper
Sauce
8 oz / 225g wild mushrooms, eg, chanterelles,
     cèpes, etc
½ oz / 15g unsalted butter
1 oz / 30g finely chopped shallot
1 small crushed clove garlic
10 floz / 300ml double cream or crème fraîche
4 oz / 115g fresh foie gras (optional)
1 dssp chopped mixed parsley & chives

Method

Roll out the puff pastry to a thickness
of ⅛" / 3mm. Cut out 4 mushroom shapes (see
illustration) & place on a greased baking
sheet; egg-wash the pastry & score so as to
create lids.

Rest in the refrigerator for about 20
minutes, then bake in an oven preheated to
400°F / 200°C / gas 6 for 15-20 minutes, until
crisp & golden-brown.

For the sauce, wash the mushrooms, season
& fry in a non-stick pan to remove all the
moisture.

Melt the butter in a separate pan & cook
the shallot & garlic until soft.

Add the cream or crème fraîche, the foie
gras, if used, & the herbs, then simmer to
reduce slightly; season to taste, add the
cooked mushrooms & simmer for 2-3 minutes.

Remove the lids from the hot pastry
cases, fill with the mushroom mixture &
serve at once.

Soufflé de sole & coquilles St. Jacques au fumet de Gewürztraminer & brunoise de legumes

LE MANOIR AUX QUAT'SAISONS
Raymond Blanc

Ingredients

Soufflé base

1 lb /450g firm scallops, the corals diced &
    reserved for the sauce
1 egg yolk
7 fl oz / 210 ml whipping cream
3 egg whites
juice of 1½ lemons
4 Dover sole fillets, each about 3 oz / 85g
1 tbsp unsalted butter
salt & freshly milled white pepper

Sauce

5 finely chopped shallots
3 tsp butter
2 oz / 60g sliced button mushrooms
bones from 2 Dover soles
7 fl oz / 210 ml Gewürztraminer
1 small finely diced carrot
1 small finely diced courgette
1 small finely diced leek
1 tbsp whipping cream
1½ oz / 45g chilled diced butter
dash lemon juice
8 finely diced white button mushrooms

Method

For the soufflés, wash the scallops,
place in a processor with the egg yolk &
1 tsp salt & purée until smooth.
Transfer to a metal bowl, refrigerate for
30 minutes, then stand over a larger bowl
containing crushed ice.
Stir in the cream, gradually at first,

then beat vigorously until it is all incorporated; pass through a fine sieve & season with pepper.

Whisk the egg whites with a pinch of salt until soft peaks form, add the juice of 1 lemon & beat until smooth.

Add one-quarter of the egg whites to the mousse using a wooden spoon, then fold in the remainder, taking care not to overmix.

Score the inner side of each sole fillet gently with a sharp knife, place between 2 sheets of clingfilm & flatten carefully with a heavy knife until 1½"/4cm wide.

Cut 4 pieces of clingfilm measuring 6"/15cm square, place a flan ring on each, wrap securely to make a false base & butter the inside of each ring.

Melt the butter with the juice of ½ lemon, season & brush on each side of the fillets.

Press the fillets around the inside of the rings, scored side inwards, ensuring that they make a full circle with no gaps.

Fill the rings with the soufflé mixture, space out in a deep roasting pan & bake in a bain-marie in an oven preheated to 450°F/230°C/gas 8 for 12 minutes.

For the sauce, soften the shallots in 2 tsp butter, add the sliced mushrooms & bones, cook for 2 minutes & add the wine.

Boil, skim, cover with 7 fl oz/210 ml water, simmer for 15 minutes, strain & reduce to 7 fl oz/210 ml.

Cook the carrot in the remaining butter & 2 fl oz/60 ml water for 2 minutes, add the courgette & leek, season & cook for 1 minute.

Add to the stock & bring back to the boil; stir in the cream, whisk in the cold diced butter, season, add a squeeze of lemon juice, stir in the diced corals & mushrooms & keep warm.

To serve, remove the soufflés from the oven, peel away the clingfilm, lift off the rings &, using a fish slice, place a soufflé on each of 4 warmed plates.

Strain any cooking juices into the sauce & pour over & around the soufflés.

Rognons de veau rôti, poêlée d'escargots, & sauce vin rouge au persil & à la Chartreuse verte

LE MANOIR AUX QUAT'SAISONS
Raymond Blanc

Ingredients

2 veal kidneys
salt & freshly milled white pepper

Sauce
1½ oz / 45g unsalted butter
2 finely chopped shallots
2 fl oz / 60ml red wine vinegar
1 sprig thyme
14 fl oz / 420ml red wine
7 fl oz / 210 ml veal jus lié (see page 149)
1 fl oz / 30ml whipping cream
1 fl oz / 30ml green chartreuse
6 drained & finely chopped snails
1 tbsp chopped parsley

Parsley
3 oz / 85g well-washed flat Italian parsley
½ oz / 15g unsalted butter
1 fl oz / 30ml whipping cream

Garnish
½ clove garlic
½ oz / 15g unsalted butter
⅓ oz / 10g finely chopped flat Italian parsley
24 drained snails, cut in half if large

Method

Prepare the kidneys: trim away the excess fat, leaving a layer about ½" / 1cm thick, cut each kidney in half lengthwise, cut out the core & season; tie each piece to retain a good shape during cooking.

Roast in a medium-sized dish in an oven preheated to 400°F / 200°C / gas 6 for 25 minutes, remove, cover loosely with aluminium foil & rest in a warm place for 15 minutes.

For the sauce, melt 1oz / 30g butter in a medium saucepan, soften the shallots for 2 or 3 minutes, deglaze with the red wine vinegar & reduce until almost evaporated.

Add the thyme & red wine, bring to the boil, skim, reduce by half & add the jus lié & cream; boil again for 1 minute, skim, add the chartreuse & simmer for 1 minute.

Rub the base of a pan with the remaining butter & sauté the snails for 1 minute: add to the sauce with the parsley, simmer for a few minutes, pass through a fine sieve into a clean saucepan, season to taste, cover & keep warm.

For the parsley, blanch in boiling salted water for 2 to 3 minutes, refresh under cold running water & drain; place in a saucepan with the butter & a little water, bring to the boil, stir in the cream, season to taste, cover & keep warm.

For the garnish, rub the base of a small frying pan with the cut clove of garlic, heat the butter, season the snails & pan-fry for 3 minutes; add the chopped parsley & keep warm.

To assemble & serve, remove the string & fat from the kidneys, slice & return to the oven for 3 minutes.

Add any juice from the kidneys to the sauce & bring back to the boil; reheat the parsley & the garnish.

Arrange the kidney slices on 4 plates, surround with the parsley, spoon the sauce around & stud with snails.

Serve immediately.

Chocoholics anonymous

MENAGE À TROIS
Antony Worrall-Thompson

These 5 dishes may be served in any combination, but are equally delicious on their own.

White chocolate mousse

Ingredients

8 oz / 225 g white chocolate
2 fl oz / 60 ml liqueur, eg Cointreau
2 tbsp coconut cream
10 fl oz / 300 ml double cream
1 egg yolk
2 oz / 60 g castor sugar
2 egg whites

Method

In a basin over hot water melt the chocolate with the liqueur, the coconut cream & 2 tbsp of the double cream; stir until smooth & remove from the heat.

Whisk the egg yolk with half the sugar until light & fluffy, then whisk into the chocolate mixture.

Whisk the rest of the cream until firm but not stiff; whisk the egg whites, slowly adding the rest of the sugar until soft peaks are formed.

Quickly but carefully fold the cream into the chocolate mixture, then the whites.

Pour into a bowl, cool in the freezer for 1 hour, then transfer to the refrigerator until ready to serve.

Dark Chocolate mousse

Ingredients

8 oz / 225 g dark chocolate
½ oz / 15 g butter
1½ fl oz / 45 ml dark rum
1½ fl oz / 45 ml banana liqueur
6 separated eggs

Method

In a basin set over hot water, slowly melt the chocolate & butter, then add the rum & banana liqueur & stir until smooth; remove from the heat.

Beat the egg yolks until light & add to the chocolate mixture, whisking until they are all incorporated.

Whisk the whites to form soft peaks, then carefully fold into the chocolate mixture.

Refrigerate for a few hours before serving.

Chocolate truffle

Ingredients

8 oz / 225 g roughly chopped Belgian chocolate
4 oz / 115 g diced unsalted butter
4 tbsp crème fraîche or sour cream
2 tbsp brandy
3 egg yolks
4 oz / 115 g icing sugar

Method

Melt the chocolate with the butter & crème fraîche or sour cream in a heavy-bottomed saucepan, stirring constantly until smooth & glossy.

Remove from the heat & stir in the brandy.

Beat the egg yolks & sugar until light, add to the chocolate mixture & whisk until smooth.

Allow to harden a little, then roll into a sausage shape in greaseproof paper & refrigerate until required.

Chocolate ice-cream with white chocolate chips

Ingredients :

8 fl oz / 240 ml single cream
6 oz / 170 g castor sugar
6 egg yolks
6 oz / 170 g dark chocolate
2 tbsp unsalted butter
16 fl oz / 450 ml double cream
few drops vanilla essence
8 oz / 225 g chopped white chocolate

Method

Heat the single cream in a heavy-bottomed saucepan.
Beat the sugar with the egg yolks until light & fluffy, pour a little hot cream on to the eggs, then add the eggs back to the pan & stir constantly over a low heat until the custard reaches a coating consistency.
Strain into a bowl & reserve.
Melt the chocolate & butter in a basin over hot water, stirring until smooth & glossy, then remove from the heat.
Slowly whisk the custard into the chocolate a little at a time until the mixture thins out.
When thoroughly blended, gradually whisk in the double cream & vanilla essence & chill.
Churn in an ice-cream machine according to the maker's instructions, or place in a domestic freezer, beating every 15 minutes to prevent the formation of ice crystals.
Fold in the white chocolate pieces after churning, or when nearly frozen.

Chocolate terrine

Ingredients

8 oz / 225 g chopped dark chocolate
3 oz / 90 g unsalted butter
6 egg yolks
1 oz / 30 g icing sugar
2 oz / 60 g cocoa powder
15 fl oz / 450 ml double cream
4 egg whites
3/4 tin black cherries

Method

In a basin set over hot water, melt the chocolate & half the butter, remove from the heat & cool slightly.

Beat the yolks with the sugar until light & fluffy.

Soften the remaining butter & cream with the cocoa powder until light.

Combine the chocolate & yolk mixtures, then add the cocoa mixture & amalgamate.

Whisk the cream until it forms soft peaks, then whisk the whites likewise.

Drain, halve & stone the cherries, then fold into the chocolate mixture.

Quickly & gently fold in the cream & whites.

Line a terrine mould with clingfilm, pour in the chocolate & cherry mixture & refrigerate until set.

To serve, put one scoop each of the white chocolate mousse, dark chocolate mousse & chocolate ice-cream on a large plate alternating with slices of both the truffle & the terrine.

Tuile of strawberries with vanilla ice-cream

MICHAEL'S NOOK
Andy Eastick

Ingredients

Ice-cream
8 fl oz / 240 ml whipping cream
few drops vanilla essence
3 egg yolks
3 oz / 85g sugar

Coulis
8 oz / 225g raspberries
2 oz / 60g sugar
juice of 1 lemon

Strawberries
12 oz / 340g strawberries
4 tbsp sugar
4 tbsp balsamic vinegar or amaretto liqueur

To serve
4 tuile baskets (see page 154)

Method

For the ice-cream, make a vanilla custard (see page 155) then strain through a fine sieve.

Either churn in an ice-cream machine according to the maker's instructions, or freeze in a freezer, beating occasionally to prevent the formation of ice crystals.

For the coulis, place the raspberries, sugar & lemon juice in a saucepan & bring to the boil over a low heat; cool, liquidise & pass through a fine sieve.

For the fruit, wash, hull & halve the strawberries & marinade for 10 minutes in the sugar & vinegar or liqueur.

To serve, pour some coulis on to 4 plates, divide the fruit between the 4 baskets, set one on each plate & top with the vanilla ice-cream.

Salmon strudel
perfumed with basil

Ingredients

4 sheets filo pastry
1 lb / 450g fresh salmon
4 sprigs fresh basil
a little seasalt
2 fl oz / 60 ml Noilly Prat or dry sherry
2 oz / 60g melted butter

Sauce

4 oz / 115g finely chopped shallot
juice of 1 lime
4 fl oz / 120 ml dry white wine
pinch sugar
4 oz / 115g unsalted butter
a little double cream (optional)
salt & cayenne pepper

Method

Fold each sheet of filo pastry in half lengthwise & lay flat.

Slice the salmon to a thickness of about 1/4"/5mm (as if carving smoked salmon), then lay the slices on the waiting pastry in a single layer.

Roughly chop the basil leaves & scatter over the salmon, then sprinkle with seasalt & a little Noilly Prat or dry sherry.

Roll up carefully as for a Swiss roll, place on a greased baking sheet & bake in an oven preheated to 400°F / 200°C / gas 6 for about 6-8 minutes until golden-brown.

For the sauce, put the shallot, lime juice, white wine & sugar into a small saucepan. bring to the boil & simmer until reduced by two-thirds.

Remove from the heat, cool slightly & add the cream, if desired.

Swirl around, adding the butter in small pieces a little at a time, & season.

To serve, coat 4 plates with the sauce & lay the strudel in slices on top.

Pan-fried veal kidneys on creamed endive with a honey & lemon sauce

MIDDLETHORPE HALL
Aidan McCormack

Ingredients

peel of 2 lemons
6½ oz / 180g unsalted butter
1 oz / 30g shallot
2 tbsp clear honey
juice of 2 lemons
10 fl oz / 300ml veal stock (see page 148)
8oz / 225g Belgian endive
4 tbsp double cream
2 lb / 900g veal kidneys
2 tbsp vegetable oil
salt & pepper

Method

Cut the lemon peel into thin strips, branch 3 times in boiling water, refresh in cold water & keep cold.

Melt 1oz / 30g butter in a saucepan, add the shallot, cook for 1 minute, then add the honey & caramelise.

Add the lemon juice, whisking all the time.

Reduce a little, then add the veal stock.

Reduce again until syrupy, then whisk in 4oz / 115g butter.

Season & strain into a clean pan, add the lemon strips & keep warm until needed.

Finely slice the endive, wash well & drain.

Melt 1oz / 30g butter in a pan, add the endive & sweat until cooked.

Add the cream & reduce until thick, then season & keep warm.

Cut the veal kidneys into ½" / 1 cm dice & season.

Heat the oil in a frying pan, add the remaining butter & melt to browning point, then add the kidneys.

Cook very quickly for 1 minute, then drain in a colander & keep warm in the oven.

Divide the endive between 4 plates, flatten slightly, add one-quarter of the kidneys to each plate, coat with the sauce & serve very hot.

Pan-fried turbot with red wine sauce served with puff-pastry parcels of spinach & mushrooms

MIDDLETHORPE HALL
Aidan McCormack

Ingredients

4 oz / 115g cooked spinach
2 oz / 60g mushrooms, cut into matchsticks
8 oz / 225g unsalted butter
4 oz / 115g puff pastry (see page 152)
1 beaten egg for egg wash
4 fillets skinned turbot, each 5 oz / 145g
2 oz / 60g chopped shallot
10 fl oz / 300 ml red wine
5 fl oz / 150 ml fish stock (see page 151)
4 fl oz / 120 ml double cream
salt 8 pepper
Garnish
fresh green herbs

Method

Fry the spinach & mushrooms in 1oz/30g butter until all the liquid has evaporated.

Remove to a plate & allow to cool.

Roll out the puff pastry to a thickness of 1/8"/3mm & cut into 4 circles, each 4"/10 cm across.

Leave to rest for 10 minutes.

Divide the spinach mixture into 4 & place one portion on half of each of the pastry circles, leaving 1/2"/1cm uncovered around the rim.

Egg-wash this rim & close the parcels, then egg-wash the tops & leave to rest for 10 minutes.

Cook in an oven preheated to 400°F/200°C/ gas 6 for about 10 minutes & keep warm until needed.

Season the turbot fillets.

Melt 1oz/30g butter in a pan, seal the turbot, cook for 3 minutes each side, remove from the pan & keep hot.

Pour off the fat, add the shallot & deglaze with red wine.

Reduce the sauce until syrupy, add the fish stock & reduce again to a syrupy consistency.

Add the cream & bring to the boil.

Cut the remaining butter into small pieces, then whisk them into the sauce & season to taste.

Spoon the sauce on to 4 hot plates & place a turbot fillet on top.

Place the puff-pastry parcels to one side of the turbot & garnish with fresh green herbs.

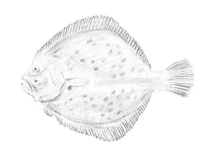

MOREL'S

Boudin de moules au beurre d'ail

Jean-Yves Morel

Ingredients

12 oz / 340g cooked mussels plus 16 for
   decoration
3 oz / 85g whiting fillet or pike, free of
   skin & bone
½ egg white
½ tbsp chopped parsley
1 crushed clove garlic
10 fl oz / 300 ml double cream
pinch nutmeg
salt & cayenne pepper
4 sausage skins

Sauce

2 oz / 60g very finely chopped shallot or
   onion
1 crushed clove garlic
6 fl oz / 180 ml dry white wine
1 tsp white wine vinegar
6 oz / 170g unsalted butter

Method

Put 8oz/225g of the mussels into a food processor with the whiting or pike & blend.

Add the egg white, blend again briefly, remove the mixture from the processor & pass through a sieve.

Place in a bowl in a refrigerator for an hour to become firm.

Chop the remaining 4oz/115g mussels & mix with the parsley & garlic.

Put some ice into a large bowl & stand the bowl containing the blended fish mixture on top of the ice.

Add the double cream a little at a time, until it is all absorbed into the mixture.

Add the chopped mussels & season with nutmeg, salt & cayenne pepper.

Soak the sausage skins in cold water for a few minutes, then drain.

Put the mussel mixture into a large piping bag with a plain nozzle, fill the skins & tie to the required length.

The sausages can be made well in advance, & kept in the refrigerator.

When ready to serve, cook gently in hot water for about 20 minutes.

For the sauce, put the chopped shallot or onion into a saucepan with the garlic, white wine & wine vinegar & reduce by three-quarters.

Strain the liquid into a clean pan.

Add to this pan small pieces of butter one at a time, swirling around the pan to make a smooth, shiny sauce.

Do not reboil.

Remove the sausages from the water, drain & serve on plates surrounded by the sauce & garnished with a few whole mussels.

Earl Grey & lemon tea parfait with mango sauce

NINETY PARK LANE
Stephen Goodlad

Ingredients

8 fl oz / 240 ml boiling water
grated rind of 2 lemons
1½ oz / 45g Earl Grey tea
4 egg yolks
5 oz / 145g soft brown sugar
4 fl oz / 120 ml milk
2 tbsp dark rum
½ vanilla pod / few drops vanilla essence
10 fl oz / 300 ml whipped double cream
2 tbsp thinly shredded mint leaves
1 tbsp lemon rind, cut into thin strips &
    blanched in boiling water

Mango sauce
3 fl oz / 90 ml water
2 oz / 60g castor sugar
1 ripe mango
juice of ½ lemon

Garnish
a few mint leaves

Method

Pour the boiling water on to the grated lemon rind & tea, leave to infuse for 5 minutes, then squeeze out the liquid through a muslin cloth.

Beat the egg yolks with the sugar until foamy.

Boil the milk, rum, vanilla (if using a pod, remove it as boiling point is reached) & tea liquor.

Take off the heat, add to the foamy eggs, return to the heat, & cook, stirring continuously, until a coating consistency is reached.

Transfer to a mixing bowl & cool completely, beating occasionally.

When the custard is the same temperature as the whipped cream, fold the latter into the mixture & add the mint & strips of lemon rind.

Pour into a rectangular terrine & freeze overnight.

For the sauce, boil the water & sugar for 5 minutes, remove from the heat & cool.

Peel the mango & roughly chop the flesh.

Blend in a liquidiser or processor with the syrup & lemon juice, then pass through a sieve.

Refrigerate until required.

To serve, unmould the terrine, slice & serve on a pool of sauce.

Garnish with mint leaves.

Serves 10.

Hot Irish Mist soufflé

PARK HOTEL
Matthew Darcy

Ingredients

3 egg yolks
finely grated rind & segments of 2 oranges
2oz / 60g sugar
1oz / 30g flour
10 fl oz/ 300ml milk
3-4 tbsp Irish Mist liqueur
5 egg whites

Method

Beat the egg yolks with the orange rind & half the sugar until thick & light, then stir in the flour.

Scald the milk, whisk into the egg mixture, blend well & return to the pan; whisk over a gentle heat until smooth, simmer for about 2 minutes, allow to cool & add the liqueur.

Whisk the egg whites until stiff, add the remaining sugar & beat until glossy, ie, about 20 seconds.

Heat the liqueur mixture until hot to the touch, remove from the heat & stir in one-quarter of the egg whites.

Add this to the remaining egg white mixture & fold together as lightly as possible.

Spoon the mixture into 8 individual or 1 large buttered & sugared soufflé dish. smooth the surface & quickly arrange the orange segments on top in a star pattern.

Bake in an oven preheated to 425°F/220°C/ gas 7 for 12-15 minutes, sprinkle with icing sugar & serve at once.

Serves 8.

Fresh mussel soup

Ingredients

2 oz / 60g finely chopped onion
1 oz / 30g butter
5 fl oz / 150ml white wine
1½ lb / 680g thoroughly cleaned mussels
2 oz / 60g leeks
2 oz / 60g celery
1 oz / 30g carrot
2 oz / 60g potato
spring marjoram
2 pt / 1 ltr fish stock (see page 151)
4 oz / 115g white fish (cod, haddock or sole)
2 fl oz / 60ml cream (optional)
salt & pepper
a little chopped parsley

Method

Sauté the onions in the butter in a large pan, add the wine & mussels, cover & shake over a high heat for 1 minute until the mussels open.

Remove the mussels & shell them, but discard any that have not opened; strain the liquor & reserve.

Chop the remaining vegetables & put into a pan with the marjoram, fish stock, fish & mussel liquor; bring to the boil, cover & simmer for 45 minutes, skimming as needed.

Remove from the heat & liquidise half the mixture; return to the pan (adjusting the consistency of the soup by combining these 2 liquids as desired), add the mussels & season to taste.

Just before serving, add a little cream, if desired, & garnish with parsley.

Pot-roast quail with Stilton mousse & muscat grape sauce

PEBBLES
David Cavalier

Ingredients

4 quail
4 oz /115g breast of chicken, free of skin &
   bone
½ egg white
5 fl oz /150 ml double cream
2 oz / 60g finely diced Stilton
2 oz / 60g butter
2 oz / 60g diced carrot
2 oz / 60g diced onion
salt & a little cayenne pepper

Rösti
2 large peeled potatoes
Salt & pepper
2 oz / 60g clarified butter

Sauce
6 fl oz / 180ml muscat wine
10 fl oz / 300 ml chicken or veal stock (see
   page 148)
8 oz / 225g peeled muscat grapes

To serve
fresh seasonal vegetables

Method

Bone the quail (or ask your butcher to do this for you).

Blend the chicken flesh in a food processor, add the egg white & gradually incorporate the cream a little at a time.

Season with salt & cayenne pepper, then remove from processor & add the Stilton.

Season the insides of the boned quails, place a little of the mousse in the centre of each, then tie with string to reshape.

Melt the butter in an oval casserole & when hot add the carrot, onion & quail, turning them to brown evenly.

Cover with a lid & cook in an oven pre-heated to 375°F / 190°C / gas 5 for 15 minutes.

For the rösti, grate the potatoes but do not rinse, then season with salt & pepper & divide into 4 circles.

Heat the clarified butter in a frying pan & fry the 4 potato circles, pressing down gently with a slice.

When the base is golden-brown, turn very carefully & transfer the pan to the oven to finish cooking; when ready, the rösti should be crisp & golden outside, & soft within.

When the quail are cooked, remove from the oven & keep warm.

For the sauce, pour the excess fat from the casserole, add the wine & boil to reduce.

Add the stock & reduce by two-thirds, strain, add the grapes & keep hot.

To serve, place a rösti potato on each plate, remove the string from the quail & set a quail on each potato cushion.

Surround with the sauce & grapes, & serve immediately with fresh seasonal vegetables.

Salmon with scallop mousseline

PLUMBER MANOR
Brian Prideaux-Brune

Ingredients

4 salmon steaks, each weighing about 8oz/
    225g
salt & cayenne pepper

Mousseline
8oz / 225g scallops
1 egg white
5 fl oz / 150ml double cream

Sauce
2oz / 60g fresh ginger
6 fl oz / 180ml fish stock (see page 151)
4 fl oz / 120ml Noilly Prat
12 fl oz / 360ml double cream
1/2 pkt saffron
1 dssp chopped fresh chives

Garnish
1 washed bunch watercress

Method

Bone the salmon steaks.

For the mousseline, blend the scallops in a food processor with the egg white.

Remove from the blender & place in a bowl set over a larger one containing crushed ice, gradually beat in the cream & season to taste.

Place the steaks on a buttered baking tray, season & fill the cavity with mousseline — this can be done in advance & the salmon kept in the refrigerator until required.

To cook, place the tray of salmon under a hot grill so that the mousse turns golden-brown on top, then finish in an oven preheated to 325°F / 170°C / gas 3 for about 15 minutes.

For the sauce, cut the ginger into slivers & put in a saucepan with the fish stock & Noilly Prat.

Bring to the boil & simmer until reduced by half.

Add the cream & saffron & reduce again until a coating consistency is reached.

Season, strain & keep hot.

To serve, add the chives to the sauce at the last moment, remove the skin from the salmon, coat 4 plates with the sauce & lay a salmon steak on each.

Garnish with watercress & serve at once.

Claire Hilti's

Hungarian goulash

POOL COURT
Melvin Jordan

Ingredients

1½ lbs / 680g good-quality stewing beef
1oz / 30g flour seasoned with paprika
1 fl oz / 30 ml olive oil
1oz / 30g butter
1½ lbs/ 680g finely chopped onion
2 cloves garlic, peeled & crushed
2 tbsp paprika
1 tbsp tomato purée
5 fl oz / 150 ml red wine
5 fl oz / 150 ml beef stock (see page 150)
1 tsp chopped mixed herbs (thyme, parsley &
   coriander)
2 whole cloves
salt

Method

Dice the meat into 1½" /4 cm cubes & roll in the seasoned flour.

Heat the oil & butter in a saucepan until very hot, add the beef & fry, turning frequently to seal the surfaces.

Add the onion & garlic, reduce heat & cook gently until the onions are completely softened.

Add the paprika & tomato purée, & cook for 10 minutes, stirring continuously.

Gradually add the red wine, & when absorbed add the stock.

Add the herbs & cloves, cover & cook in an oven preheated to 350°F / 180°C / gas 4 for 1½-2 hours.

Check that the sauce does not become too dry during cooking, adding more wine or stock if necessary. However, make sure the sauce is not too thin. Check seasoning.

When the meat is tender, serve with pasta, rice or spätzli.

Calves' liver with avocado

POOL COURT
Melvin Jordan

Ingredients

4 oz / 115 g unsalted butter
8 slices calves' liver, each 3 oz / 85 g
16 chopped fresh sage leaves
10 fl oz / 300 ml dry white wine
juice of ½ lemon
1 avocado

Method

Melt 1 oz / 30 g butter in a large shallow frying pan.

Fry the slices of liver gently for about 1 minute each side, then remove & keep warm.

Add the sage leaves & wine to the pan & stir well, scraping up the residue.

When the liquor has reduced slightly, whisk in the rest of the butter in small pieces, then add the lemon juice.

Simmer until the sauce has a light coating consistency.

Meanwhile, skin & stone the avocado, cut into thin slices & warm gently under the grill.

To serve, arrange the liver on plates, pour the sauce over, & top with avocado slices.

Kumquat ice-cream

Ingredients

6 oz / 170 g kumquats
3 oz / 85 g marmalade
2 oz / 60 g sugar
juice & zest of 1 orange
juice & zest of 1 lemon
2 egg yolks
5 fl oz / 150 ml milk
1 tbsp glucose
8 fl oz / 240 ml double cream
8 tuile baskets (see page 154)
1 segmented orange
8 sprigs mint

Method

Wash the kumquats, cut in half, remove
the seeds & slice thinly; place in a
saucepan with the marmalade & half the
sugar & caramelise over a low heat.

Remove from the heat & carefully stir in
the orange & lemon juices & zests; allow to
cool but not to go completely cold.

Meanwhile, beat the egg yolks lightly
with the milk, glucose & remaining sugar;
stir over a low heat until the mixture
thickens, but do not allow it to boil.

Remove from the heat, strain immediately
on to the kumquat mixture & stir well.

Allow to cool completely, add the double
cream & freeze, either in an ice-cream
machine according to the maker's
instructions, or in a freezer, beating
every 15 minutes to prevent the formation
of ice crystals.

To serve, scoop the ice-cream into the
tuile baskets & garnish with orange
segments & mint sprigs.

Serves 8.

Princess scallops with saffron

Christopher Trotter
Portsonachan Hotel

Ingredients

40 Princess scallops, or 2 lb / 900 g Venus
  clams
1 sprig parsley
1 sprig thyme
½ bay leaf
8 peppercorns
5 fl oz / 150 ml dry white wine
5 fl oz / 150 ml fish stock (see page 151)
1 packet saffron
2½ fl oz / 75 ml double cream
chopped parsley
salt & pepper

Method

Wash the scallops or clams in cold water & make sure they are all tightly closed; discard any with broken shells.

Put the herbs & peppercorns into a saucepan, add the scallops or clams & the wine, cover & cook gently over low heat until they all open.

Remove the scallops or clams to a dish & keep warm, discarding any that have not opened.

Add the fish stock to the pan & boil until the liquid is reduced by half.

Add the saffron & the cream, & reduce slightly to a thin, creamy consistency.

Season to taste & add the chopped parsley.

Put the scallops or clams into soup bowls, pour over the hot liquid & serve immediately.

Princess scallops are very small scallops farmed in Scotland. They are not easily found in other parts of the country, but Venus clams are equally delicious cooked in the same way & are easier to find.

Terrine of leeks & foie gras

LE POUSSIN
Alex Aitken

Ingredients

16 small leeks
9 oz / 250g butter
9 oz / 250g fresh foie gras
salt & pepper

Sauce
4 floz / 120 ml double cream
2 oz / 60g chilled, diced unsalted butter

Method

Clean & trim the leeks, reserving the best trimmings for the sauce, soak in cold water, wash thoroughly to remove any soil, then cut to the same length as your chosen terrine mould.

Place the leeks in a saucepan large enough to take them lengthwise, just cover with water, season & add the butter.

Bring quickly to the boil, turn off the heat & let them cool in their own juices.

Cut the foie gras into slices 1/2" / 1 cm thick.

Heat a thick-bottomed frying pan until smoking, but do not add any oil or butter.

Quickly sear the foie gras slices for 4 seconds on each side, then remove to a cold plate & reserve any fat that has exuded from them during cooking.

Line a terrine mould with cling film, pressing it well into the corners.

Drain but do not dry the leeks, reserving the cooking liquor for the sauce.

Put a layer of leeks in the terrine, pushing them well down to cover the entire

base (depending on width you will need 3 or 4 leeks per layer).

Place half the foie gras slices with half the reserved fat on top of the leeks & season.

Repeat with another layer of leeks, another of foie gras & a final layer of leeks.

For a prettier final presentation, vary the green & white parts of the leeks at each end of the terrine.

Refrigerate for at least 12 hours.

For the sauce, cut the reserved leek trimmings into thin strips 1" / 2 cm long.

Reduce the liquid in which the leeks were poached by two-thirds, add the leek strips & cream, then whisk in the butter.

To serve, carefully turn out the terrine & lift off & discard the cling film.

Using a very sharp knife, cut the terrine into slices 1" / 2 cm thick, place on warm plates & surround with the sauce.

Warm vegetable salad with grilled Yarg

READ'S
Norman Cook

Ingredients

4 small courgettes
1 medium aubergine
4 small leeks
4 baby sweetcorn
4 okra
1 red pimento
3 floz / 90 ml olive oil
juice of 1 lemon
chopped leaves of 1 sprig thyme
4 pieces Yarg cheese, each 3oz / 85g
4 leaves radicchio
salt & pepper

Method

Wash the vegetables; cut the courgettes & aubergine into slices ¼" / 5mm thick, trim the leeks, leaving a small amount of green leaf still attached, leave the sweetcorn & okra whole, & quarter the pimento, removing the core & seeds.

Blanch the vegetables in a large pot of boiling, salted water for 2-3 minutes, remove, drain & put into iced water.

Make a dressing with the oil, lemon juice & thyme, then season.

Wrap each piece of cheese in a radicchio leaf.

Drain & dry the vegetables, brush lightly with oil & place under a hot grill until just cooked but still crunchy.

At the same time, grill the cheese parcels.

Toss the vegetables in the dressing, set each cheese parcel on a warmed plate & surround with the dressed vegetables.

Read's likes to use English ingredients, & this unusual Cornish cheese, matured in nettle leaves, is featured as a vegetarian dish, a starter, & a warm cheese course.

Walnut tart with rhubarb

READ'S
Norman Cook

Ingredients

6oz / 170g sweet pastry (see page 153)
2 lb / 900g rhubarb
10 fl oz / 300 ml sugar syrup (see page 154)
10 fl oz / 300 ml fresh vanilla custard (see
  page 155)
4 oz / 115g sugar
8 oz / 225g shelled walnuts
10 fl oz / 300 ml double cream
4 sprigs mint

Method

Line 4 tartlet cases with a thin layer of
sweet pastry & bake blind in an oven
preheated to 375°F / 190°C / gas 5 for 10-15
minutes.
Wash the rhubarb, cut into 1" / 3 cm
lengths, stew in the sugar syrup, then
drain.
Pureé half the rhubarb & mix with the
vanilla custard to make ice-cream.
If you have an ice-cream machine, churn
according to the maker's instructions; if
not, place in a freezer until frozen,
beating every 15 minutes to prevent the
formation of ice-crystals.
Boil the sugar with a little water until
golden-brown, add the walnuts, coating them
well in the caramel, then the cream & cook
until all the caramel has dissolved.
Divide the mixture between the tartlet
shells.
Place a tartlet on each of 4 plates, top
with a scoop of rhubarb ice-cream & spoon
the remaining rhubarb around.
Garnish with a sprig of mint.

Sauté of rabbit with apples & calvados

RESTAURANT 19
Stephen Smith

Ingredients

1 rabbit

Marinade
5 fl oz / 150 ml dry white wine
4 oz / 115g sliced carrot
4 oz / 115g sliced onion
1 clove garlic
3 sprigs thyme
1 bay leaf
2 fl oz / 60 ml olive oil
2 fl oz / 60 ml white wine vinegar
salt & pepper

Cooking & garnish
4 oz / 115g clarified butter
1 lb / 450g Golden Delicious apples
3 fl oz / 90 ml calvados
10 fl oz / 300 ml rabbit stock (see method)
2 oz / 60g butter
few sprigs chervil or parsley

Method

Prepare the rabbit: cut the legs from the body, the fillets from the saddle, then roughly chop the carcass.

Bone out the legs, & remove any fat & sinew from the flesh.

Use all the bones to make a good stock (see basic method on page 148).

Mix the ingredients for the marinade, pour over the rabbit in an earthenware dish & leave overnight.

To cook, heat half the clarified butter in a pan, add the rabbit legs & colour lightly on all sides.

Place the pan in an oven preheated to 350°F/180°C/ gas 4 for 5 minutes.

Remove from the oven, add the rabbit fillets, colour on all sides & return to the oven for about 10-15 minutes.

Meanwhile, peel, core & slice the apples & sauté in the remaining clarified butter.

When the rabbit is cooked, remove from the oven & keep warm.

Pour the excess fat from the pan & deglaze with Calvados.

Boil to reduce slightly, add the rabbit stock, boil again & reduce by half.

Gradually add the 2oz/60g butter, & check seasoning.

To serve, arrange the apples on plates & place the rabbit legs on top.

Slice the fillets lengthwise & arrange at the side of the plate.

Chop the chervil or parsley, add to the sauce & pour over the rabbit.

Passion-fruit mousse with passion-fruit sauce

RESTAURANT 19
Stephen Smith

Ingredients

8 passion fruit

Sauce

10 fl oz / 300ml water
8 oz / 225g sugar
½ tsp gelatine

Mousse

5 egg yolks
2 oz / 60g sugar
10 fl oz / 300 ml milk
½ vanilla pod or a few drops vanilla
    essence
½ tbsp gelatine
5 fl oz / 150 ml whipping cream

Garnish

4 passion fruit

Method

Remove the flesh from the passion-fruit shells & sieve to remove seeds; reserve the resulting juice.

For the sauce, boil the water & sugar together for 5 minutes, add the passion-fruit shells & simmer gently.

After about 15 minutes squeeze the shells between 2 spoons to give the sauce flavour & a pink colour, then strain the sauce.

Dissolve the gelatine in 4 tbsp of the sauce, then pour into the base of either one large (1pt / 500ml) or 4 small (5fl oz / 150ml) moulds & allow to set.

For the mousse, beat the egg yolks with the sugar in a basin until pale & creamy.

Heat the milk with the vanilla & pour gently on to the eggs, whisking all the time; return to the pan & cook gently until a coating consistency is reached.

Remove from the heat.

Dissolve the gelatine in a little cold water, add to the custard & allow to cool.

Lightly whip the cream, fold into the custard with the passion-fruit juice, pour into the prepared moulds (ie, on top of the prepared set syrup) & refrigerate until set.

To serve, dip the moulds into hot water for a few seconds & turn out on to a serving plate.

Surround with the remaining sauce & garnish with one passion fruit per person, cut in half.

Passion fruit are of similar size & shape to a plum, with a hard purple skin that becomes crinkly as the fruit inside ripens.

The orange flesh is aromatic, sweet & juicy, & full of little black edible seeds. It may be simply eaten with a teaspoon, or scooped out & used in a variety of recipes, such as this one.

Loin or shoulder of pork with red cabbage

RESTAURANT ROGER BURDELL

Ingredients

2 lb / 900g piece of boned, rindless, rolled
   loin or shoulder of pork
5 fl oz / 150ml sour cream
salt & pepper
Cooked marinade
4 oz / 115g roughly chopped onion
4 oz / 115g roughly chopped leek
4 oz / 115g roughly chopped celery
4 oz / 115g roughly chopped carrot
1 pt / 500ml red or white wine
5 fl oz / 150ml wine vinegar
2 oz / 60g sugar
2 bay leaves
3 crushed cloves
1 dssp thyme leaves
6 crushed juniper berries
10 crushed black peppercorns
Red cabbage
2 oz / 60g butter
1 thinly sliced large onion
1¼ lb / 550g finely sliced red cabbage
1 large peeled & sliced cooking apple
1 oz / 30g brown sugar
10 fl oz / 300ml white wine
1 fl oz / 30ml wine vinegar
3 juniper berries & 2 cloves, tied in a
   piece of muslin

Method

Tie the pork so that it retains its shape during cooking.

For the marinade, put all the ingredients in a saucepan, bring to the boil, then allow to go cold.

Place the meat in the marinade for 4 or 5 days, turning occasionally, then drain, reserving the marinade.

Season the meat & brown on all sides in a hot pan, then transfer to an oven preheated to 375 °F / 190 °C / gas 5 for about 1½ hours.

For the cabbage, melt the butter in a saucepan, soften the onion, add the cabbage & remaining ingredients, bring to the boil & simmer, covered, for about 30 minutes.

Remove the juniper berries & cloves.

When the meat is cooked remove from the oven & keep hot.

Drain off the fat, add 10 fl oz / 300 ml of the marinade to the pan, bring to the boil & simmer for 10 minutes.

Add the sour cream, bring back to the boil, simmer for a further 10 minutes, then strain.

To serve, slice the meat, arrange on 4 plates with the cabbage to one side & hand the sauce separately; freshly cooked noodles go well with this dish.

Roger Burdell says that coming as he does from a family of Nottinghamshire & Lincolnshire pork butchers, & having also spent a number of years in Germany, the versatility of pork seems simply a way of life. This particular dish has its inspiration in the cooking of southern Germany, where the meat is often merely a means to enjoying a plateful of noodles, swimming in a delicious, sharp creamy sauce.

Iced rhubarb soufflé with elderflower & orange

RESTAURANT ROGER BURDELL

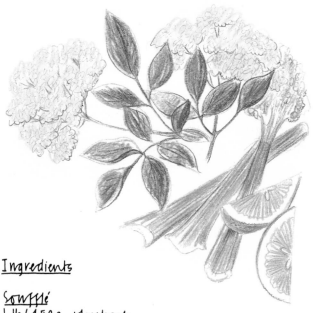

Ingredients

Soufflé
1 lb / 450g rhubarb
10 fl oz / 300ml elderflower cordial
(see note at end of recipe)
8 oz / 225g castor sugar
5 fl oz / 150ml egg white
14 fl oz / 420ml whipping cream

Fruit
1 lb / 450g rhubarb
10 fl oz / 300ml elderflower cordial (see notes)
2 peeled & segmented oranges

Method

For the soufflé, wash the rhubarb, cut into 1" / 3 cm lengths, poach in the elderflower cordial, then purée - you need 10 fl oz / 300 ml purée.

Put the castor sugar into a saucepan with a little water, bring to the boil & cook until it reaches the 'hard ball' stage, ie, 250°F / 120°C

Meanwhile, whisk the egg white until stiff.

Pour the boiling sugar into the egg white, whisking continuously until it is all incorporated.

Allow to cool.

Lightly whip the cream, fold it into the rhubarb purée, then fold in the cooled meringue.

Pour into a soufflé dish or bombe mould & freeze for 24 hours.

For the fruit, wash the rhubarb & cut into 1" / 3cm lengths.

Very gently bring to simmering point in the cordial, then remove from the heat.

Allow to cool, then just before serving add the orange segments.

To serve, turn out the soufflé & spoon the rhubarb & oranges around it.

Serves 8.

Note: to make elderflower cordial, collect elderflower heads when full blown & place in a large saucepan with plenty of strong sugar syrup. Add some gooseberries if available, as they will greatly improve the flavour. Boil, cool, strain & store in sterilised bottles. Alternatively, the cordial may be purchased in London at Neal's Yard, WC2.

Smoked salmon strudel

ROGER'S RESTAURANT
Roger Pergl-Wilson

Ingredients

2 eggs
3 oz / 85g smoked salmon
2 oz / 60g white mushrooms
3 oz / 85g butter
10 fl oz / 300 ml double cream
1 tsp flour
1 dssp chopped chives
4 leaves filo pastry
salt & cayenne pepper
Garnish
1 bunch watercress
French dressing

Method

Hard-boil the eggs. Cool in cold water, shell & chop finely.

Cut the smoked salmon into ¼"/5mm dice & add to the eggs.

Chop the mushrooms into similar dice, & cook in 1oz/30g of the butter in a saucepan until soft.

Add the cream & bring to the boil.

Mix a teaspoonful of butter into a paste with the flour & whisk this into the cream & mushrooms until the mixture thickens.

Stir in the eggs, salmon & chives, season to taste & allow to cool.

Melt the remaining butter.

Lay a sheet of filo pastry on a dry, clean, flat surface & brush it with some of the melted butter.

Fold over in half to create a double layer.

Repeat with the remaining 3 sheets of pastry.

Place equal quantities of the salmon mixture on the end of each sheet, fold in the sides & roll up to resemble Swiss roll shapes.

Bake in an oven preheated to 400°F/ 200°C/gas 6 for about 15 minutes, until crisp & golden.

Serve immediately, garnished with the washed watercress tossed in the French dressing.

Salad of English ewes' milk cheese, tomato & herbs

RULE'S
Nick Steiger

Ingredients

2 small Mendip Hills ewes' milk cheeses
4 skinned tomatoes
4 fl oz / 120 ml olive oil
1 fl oz / 30 ml white wine vinegar
1 tbsp chopped fresh herbs, eg, any one or
more from basil, tarragon, chives,
marjoram, chervil & parsley
salt & pepper
4 sprigs watercress for garnish

Method

Slice each cheese into 6 & each tomato
into 3.
Make a dressing with the oil & vinegar,
season to taste, add the herbs & beat well.
To serve, lay 3 pieces of cheese on each
plate, top each piece with a slice of
tomato & at the last moment coat with the
dressing, making sure that the salad is
well covered with herbs.
Garnish each serving with a sprig of
watercress.

Summer pudding

RULE'S

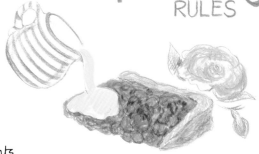

Ingredients

- 4-6oz / 115-170g sliced crustless white bread
- 1 lb / 450g fresh seasonal berries, e.g. strawberries, raspberries, cherries, blueberries, blackberries, redcurrants (try to use one-quarter strawberries, one-quarter raspberries & 2 others)
- 1 floz / 30ml water
- 5oz / 145g sugar

To serve

best Jersey double cream

Method

Line the base & sides of a 1½ pt / 750ml pudding basin with most of the bread.

Wash the chosen fruit, then run or stone.

Put the water & sugar in a saucepan & bring slowly to the boil.

Add the prepared fruit & cook for a few minutes, ensuring that the fruit retains its shape.

Drain off most of the syrup & reserve.

Cool the fruit, spoon into the prepared basin & top with a further slice of bread.

Pour over a little of the juice, cover with a plate & place a weight on top.

Refrigerate for at least 24 hours. Carefully unmould & pour over the reserved juice.

Serve with the cream.

Iced hazelnut mousse

Francis Coulson
Sharrow Bay

Ingredients

Praline
4oz / 115g castor sugar
1 fl oz / 30 ml water
4oz / 115g roasted, roughly chopped hazelnuts

Mousse
6 egg whites
9oz / 250g castor sugar
7 fl oz / 210 ml double cream
10 fl oz / 300 ml single cream

Sauce
9oz / 250g raspberries
3oz / 85g castor sugar
juice of 1/2 lemon

Method

For the praline, boil the sugar with the water in a saucepan.

When the sugar begins to turn golden brown, stir in the hazelnuts & pour the mixture on to an oiled tray.

Allow to go cold, then lightly crush into small pieces using a rolling pin on greaseproof paper.

For the mousse, whisk the egg whites & sugar in a bowl over a pan of hot water until the sugar dissolves.

Remove from the heat & whisk until cold.

Mix the double & single creams & whisk them until they thicken slightly.

Fold the cream into the egg & sugar mixture with the praline.

Pour into a rectangular tin lined with wax paper & freeze overnight.

For the sauce, liquidise the raspberries with the sugar, add lemon juice to taste & strain to remove seeds.

To serve, remove the iced mousse from the tin, cut into slices & serve on top of the sauce.

Makes 12 portions.

Medallions of veal with port wine sauce & onion marmalade

SHARROW BAY
Francis Coulson

Ingredients

Onion marmalade
3 medium-sized onions
4 oz / 115g butter
4 tbsp veal stock
4 tbsp dry white wine
4 tbsp sweet sherry
2 tbsp sherry vinegar
½ tsp salt
½ oz / 15g sugar
6 fl oz / 180 ml double cream

Garnish
4 oz / 115g peeled button onions
4 oz / 115g peeled baby carrots
4 oz / 115g peeled baby turnips
3 oz / 85g butter
1 dssp chopped parsley

Medallions & sauce
1 oz / 30g clarified butter
4 veal medallions, each 6 oz / 170g
6 fl oz / 180 ml port
6 fl oz / 180 ml brown veal stock (see page 148)
salt & pepper

Method

For the onion marmalade, slice the onions very thinly & cook gently in a saucepan with 2oz/60g butter for about 30 minutes, stirring frequently, until soft.

Add the stock, wine, sherry, sherry vinegar, salt & sugar, & simmer gently until all the liquid has evaporated.

Put the cream in another pan, simmer until thick, add the onions, mix well & keep warm.

For the garnish, cook the button onions, carrots & turnips in a little salted water with the butter, so that they acquire a glaze.

When cooked, sprinkle with chopped parsley.

For the medallions, heat the clarified butter in a frying pan.

When hot, season the medallions, add to the pan & cook until just done - about 3-5 minutes each side.

Remove from the pan & keep warm.

Deglaze the pan with the port & reduce over a high heat until syrupy.

Add the veal stock & reduce by half.

Over a low heat, gradually whisk in the remaining butter, check seasoning & strain.

Divide the onion marmalade between 4 plates, placing it centrally; set a veal medallion on each portion, pour the sauce around & garnish with the glazed vegetables.

Serve immediately.

Pot au feu de saumon au gros sel

LE SOUFFLÉ
Peter Kromberg

Ingredients

the marrow from 1 beef bone - optional
1lb / 450g new Jersey potatoes
8 peeled baby carrots
4 baby leeks, cut to 3" / 6 cm length
½ a celeriac root, peeled & cut into wedges
1 medium bulb fennel, cut into quarters
1 floz / 30ml virgin olive oil
1 tbsp seasalt
4 boned salmon steaks, each 4oz / 115g, with
    skin on
1½ pt / 650 ml court bouillon (see page   )
juice of 1 large lemon
16 peeled cherry tomatoes
1 bunch fresh chervil

Method

If using, soak the bone marrow in cold water overnight.

The next day, bring the bone marrow to boil in salt water, simmer for 5 minutes, remove & cool.

Wash the potatoes, steam & peel them.

Prepare & cook the carrots, leeks, celeriac & fennel individually in lightly salted water, avoiding overcooking.

Lightly oil the bottom of a large, shallow casserole, sprinkle with half the salt & lay the salmon steaks in it.

Place the marrow & all the vegetables except the tomatoes around the fish.

Add the cold court bouillon & bring to the boil.

Remove from the heat, cover & allow to stand for 5 minutes.

Arrange the salmon, marrow & vegetables on a serving dish, cover with foil & keep warm.

Reduce the cooking liquor by half, strain & blend, adding olive oil & lemon juice to taste.

Pour into a saucepan, add the tomatoes & chopped chervil, bring to the boil & pour over the salmon & vegetables.

Sprinkle the remaining salt over the fish & serve immediately.

Note: For court bouillon, put into a saucepan 1¼ pt / 650 ml water, 3 fl oz / 90 ml white wine vinegar, 1 each small thinly sliced carrot, onion & stick celery, 1 sprig thyme, 1 small bayleaf & a few parsley stalks; bring to the boil, add a little salt & a few peppercorns; simmer for 20 minutes; strain, cool & use as required.

Les pilons de volaille à la vapeur au basilic & aux ravioles

LE SOUFFLÉ
Peter Kromberg

Ingredients

Ravioli dough
7 oz / 200g strong flour
pinch salt
2 egg yolks & 1 whole egg, beaten together
1 tbsp olive oil

Ravioli filling
2 oz / 60g chopped chicken livers
4 chopped chicken hearts & kidneys
4 chopped chicken gizzards
1 oz / 30g softened butter
2 oz / 60g finely chopped cooked mushrooms
1½ oz / 45g white breadcrumbs
chopped leaves of 1 sprig thyme

Chicken
4 chicken legs (from corn-fed birds)
1 finely chopped shallot
3 fl oz / 90ml dry white wine
1 oz / 30g butter
4 oz / 115g finely diced mixed carrot, celery
   & onion
1 oz / 30g fresh or rehydrated morel mushrooms
2 fl oz / 60ml Madeira wine
2 oz / 60g minced chicken
1½ oz / 45g fresh foie gras
4 peeled baby carrots
35 fl oz / 1 ltr chicken stock
1 bunch fresh basil
1 oz / 30g butter, cooked to a pale roux with
   1 oz / 30g flour
juice of 1 lemon
2 fl oz / 60ml olive oil
2 peeled, seeded & quartered ripe tomatoes
seasalt & freshly milled white pepper

134

Method

For the dough, sieve the flour & salt into a bowl, add the eggs & oil & mix, adding a little cold water if necessary.

Allow to rest in a cool place for at least 30 minutes before rolling out.

For the filling, mix all the ingredients together & season.

Roll out the ravioli dough thinly, make into ravioli with the filling in the usual way & keep in the refrigerator until required.

For the chicken, bone out the legs & marinade for 3-4 hours with the shallot, white wine & freshly milled white pepper.

Melt the butter in a small saucepan, add the finely diced root vegetables, morels & Madeira, cook for a few minutes, season, cool completely, then mix with the minced chicken & foie gras.

Take the chicken legs from the marinade & place a baby carrot inside each to serve as a drumstick.

Fill the legs with the stuffing, pulling the skin around to seal, & wrap each in a small piece of muslin.

Poach the ravioli in the chicken stock for 5 minutes, then drain & reserve.

Wash the basil & remove the leaves from the stalks.

Add the stalks to the stock & bring back to the boil; steam the chicken legs in the vapour from the stock for about 30 minutes, then remove & keep warm.

Thicken the stock with the roux, boil for a few minutes, add the lemon juice & olive oil, then strain.

Shred the basil leaves & add to the sauce with the ravioli & tomatoes.

Remove the muslin from the cooked legs, place each in a soup plate, surround with the ravioli & tomatoes, pour the sauce over & serve at once.

Sea·bass with olives

LA TANTE CLAIRE
Pierre Koffman

Ingredients

4 sea-bass escalopes, each about 5oz / 145g
3 fl oz / 90ml fish stock (see page 151)
salt & pepper

Stuffing

11oz / 310g finely chopped Paris mushrooms
1 finely chopped shallot
1oz / 30g butter
4oz / 115g seeded & finely chopped red pepper
2 tbsp chopped parsley
few drops olive oil

Sauce

11 oz / 310 g tomatoes
4 fl oz / 120 ml olive oil
1 finely chopped shallot
12 peeled cloves garlic
16 black olives
16 green olives
1 tbsp chopped fresh herbs (basil, chives or chervil)

Method

Wash, trim & pat dry the sea-bass escalopes & lay them skin side down in a shallow baking dish.

For the stuffing, cook the mushrooms & shallot in the butter until soft.

Combine the cooked mushroom & shallot mixture with the red pepper, chopped parsley & olive oil, then season with salt & pepper.

Divide the stuffing between the 4 escalopes, taking care not to overfill. Pour the fish stock around the sea bass and bake for about 8 minutes in an oven preheated to 400°F / 200°C / gas 6.

For the sauce, blanch the tomatoes in boiling water for a few seconds, plunge into cold & skin them; remove the seeds & roughly chop the flesh.

Heat 1 fl oz / 30 ml of the olive oil in a saucepan, add the shallot & tomatoes & cook gently, covered, for about 15 minutes.

Remove from the heat & blend in a liquidiser or processor.

Blanch the garlic cloves in boiling water, drain & fry in the remaining olive oil until golden; drain & add to the sauce.

Stone & roughly chop the olives & add to the sauce with the herbs, salt & pepper.

To serve, pour some tomato coulis on to 4 warmed plates, set a sea-bass escalope on top & serve at once.

Stuffed breast of chicken flamed in Pernod

Thornbury Castle
Colin Hingston

<u>Ingredients</u>

1 oz / 30g finely chopped onion, softened in
  butter
3 oz / 85g raw chicken
zest & juice of 1 lime
4 oz / 115g roasted, peeled & chopped
hazelnuts
1 egg
4 oz / 115g fresh breadcrumbs
4 boned & skinned chicken breasts
1 fl oz / 30 ml Pernod
5 fl oz / 150 ml double cream
salt & pepper

Method

Put the onion, raw chicken, lime zest & juice, nuts, egg & breadcrumbs into a food processor & blend to a fairly coarse mixture.

Cut a pocket in each chicken breast, remove the loose fillets from the back of the breasts & flatten them out.

Season the breasts, put some stuffing into each pocket & cover with the fillet.

Roll into a neat shape & wrap in buttered aluminium foil.

Bake in an oven preheated to 400 °F/ 200°C / gas 6 for about 20 minutes

Remove from the foil, sprinkle with Pernod & flame.

Put the juices from the foil into a pan with the cream & a little more Pernod, & boil until reduced to a thickish sauce.

Coat the breasts with the sauce & serve immediately.

Saffron rice or buttered pasta would go well with this dish.

Bresaola

WALNUT TREE INN
Franco Taruschio

Ingredients

5 lb / 2.25 kg topside of beef
1¼ pt / 700 ml red wine
1¼ pt / 700 ml white wine
1 lb 10 oz / 750g coarse seasalt
1 large bunch rosemary
24 cloves
12 bay leaves
40 black peppercorns
3 crushed cloves garlic
4 strips orange peel
12 dry chillies

To serve

best virgin olive oil
roughly ground black pepper
lemon wedges

Method

Trim the fat & sinews from the topside & place it in a plastic or earthenware container.

Cover with the other ingredients & leave to marinade in a cool place for about a week, or until firm to the touch.

When ready, hang in a dry, airy place for another week, or until the meat feels firm enough to be sliced very thinly.

Rub with olive oil, wrap in greaseproof paper & store in the refrigerator until required.

To serve, slice very thinly (like Parma ham) & dress with best virgin olive oil, roughly ground black pepper & a wedge of lemon.

Note: although this is an expensive preparation, it is far superior to & cheaper than that sold in a delicatessen.

Brodetto

Ingredients

3 lb / 1.35 kg mixed fish, to include 12 oz / 340g
   squid, the remainder being a mixture of
   red mullet, monkfish, scampi, mussels,
   sole, whiting or gurnard
12 oz / 340g plum tomatoes (tinned if fresh
   are not available)
2 fl oz / 60ml olive oil
3 oz / 85g finely chopped onion
1 crushed clove garlic
8 oz / 225g peeled, seeded & chopped tomatoes
5 fl oz / 150ml dry white wine
1 fl oz / 30ml white wine vinegar
1 tbsp chopped parsley
Salt & pepper
To serve
hot toast

Method

Prepare the fish: cut the cleaned squid
into rings, clean the mussels & remove the
beards, then cut the remaining fish into
equal-sized pieces so that they will all
cook evenly.

Pulp the plum tomatoes in a blender or
processor, then sieve to remove the seeds.

Heat the olive oil in a shallow casserole
large enough to hold all the ingredients &
fry the onion & garlic until golden.

Add the squid & cook for a few minutes,
then add the chopped tomatoes, white wine &
white vinegar.

Add the sieved plum tomatoes, the thicker
pieces of fish, then the smaller ones.

Add a little water, season to taste,
cover the pan & cook until just done-
about 10 minutes.

Remove from the heat & leave to settle
for a few minutes, still uncovered.

Meanwhile, make the hot toast.

Sprinkle the brodetto with chopped
parsley & serve with the toast.

Pigeonneaux au coulis de pêches

THE WATERSIDE INN
Michel Roux

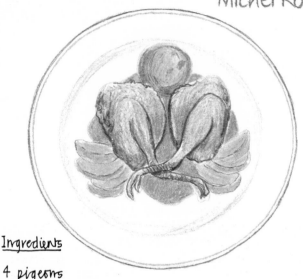

Ingredients

4 pigeons
4 oz / 115g butter
1 tbsp oil
5 white peaches
1 oz / 30g icing sugar
pinch castor sugar
2 peeled & finely chopped shallots
3 tbsp cognac
3 tbsp Grand Marnier
7 fl oz / 210 ml veal stock (see page 150)
7 fl oz / 210 ml chicken stock (see page 148)
salt & pepper

Method

Salt the insides of the pigeons & smear the outsides with 1oz / 30g melted butter.
Sauté in hot oil over a high heat, browning on all sides, then transfer to an oven preheated to 450 °F/ 230 °C/ gas 8 for 12 minutes.

When done, at which stage the breasts should still be pink in the centre, remove from the oven to a plate & keep warm.

Peel the peaches by plunging them first into boiling water. Then into cold to refresh.

Cut them in half & remove the stones, reserving those & the skins.

Soften 8 of the peach halves in 1½ oz / 50g melted butter for 1 minute — they should still be crisp.

Sprinkle with icing sugar, glaze under a very hot grill, then reserve at room temperature.

Cut off the pigeon's legs, remove the thigh bones & return the legs to the oven for a further 3 minutes.

Carve off the breasts, reserve at room temperature & chop the carcasses.

Pour the fat from the roasting tray & set over a high heat.

Add the castor sugar & brown the shallots, carcasses, peach skins, stones & 2 remaining peach halves.

Deglaze the pan with the cognac & Grand Marnier, reduce the liquid by two-thirds & add the veal & chicken stocks.

Simmer over a gentle heat for 20 minutes, skimming occasionally.

Strain through a conical sieve, return to the pan & reduce until slightly syrupy; correct the seasoning with salt & pepper, stir in the remaining butter a little at a time & keep warm.

Meanwhile, reduce the oven temperature to 325 °F / 170 °C / gas 3.

Arrange 2 breasts in the centre of each of 4 ovenproof plates with a leg & a peach half on either side & return to the oven for 4 minutes.

Remove from the oven, pour the hot sauce over the pigeons & serve immediately.

Note: a drop of Angostura bitters will add a little extra 'something' to the sauce of this delicate & many-flavoured dish.

Tarte al' coloche

THE WATERSIDE INN
Michel Roux

<u>Ingredients</u>

7 oz / 200 g flour
4 oz / 115 g slightly softened butter
1 small lightly beaten egg
pinch sugar
3/4 tsp salt
1 dssp milk

<u>Filling</u>

12 medium Cox's apples
1/2 cinnamon stick or a pinch ground cinnamon
4 turns of the pepper mill
4 oz / 115 g butter
5 oz / 145 g sugar
1 pt / 500 ml double cream
2 eggs

<u>Method</u>

   <u>For the pastry</u>, place the flour on a work
surface & make a well in the centre.
   Cut the butter into small pieces, place
in the well together with the egg, sugar &
salt, then rub in with the fingertips of
the right hand, drawing in the flour a
little at a time.

When mostly incorporated add the cold milk & knead with the heel of the hand until completely homogeneous, taking care not to handle too much.

Wrap in greaseproof paper or polythene & chill in the refrigerator for several hours before using.

When ready to make the tart, roll out the pastry on a lightly floured surface to a thickness of about 1/8" / 3 mm.

Grease a flan ring, place on a baking sheet, line with the pastry & trim off any excess.

Lightly crimp the edges to give a frilled effect above the edge of the ring, then rest in the refrigerator for at least 20 minutes.

Line the pastry with greaseproof paper, fill with baking beans & bake blind in an oven preheated to 425°F / 220°C / gas 7 for 20 minutes, or until half cooked.

Remove the paper & beans, reserve the pastry case in a warm place & reduce the oven temperature to 400°F / 200°C / gas 6.

For the filling, peel, core & quarter the apples, place one-third in a saucepan with 2 tbsp water & the cinnamon, cover & cook gently until soft.

Remove the cinnamon stick, if used, add the pepper, beat vigorously to a purée & reserve at room temperature.

Melt the butter in a large, thick-bottomed pan, immediately add the sugar & cook gently to a pale caramel.

Add the remaining apple quarters & roll in the caramel for 4 minutes — they should be cooked but still firm.

Remove the apples & reserve, pour the caramel into a bowl, stir in the cream & eggs & beat lightly.

Spread the purée over the base of the pastry case & arrange the apple quarters on top.

Pour the caramel mixture over the apples & bake for 25 minutes.

Sprinkle lightly with icing sugar, if desired, & serve warm.

Arbroath smokie hotpots

WHITE MOSS HOUSE
Peter Dixon

Ingredients

2 flaked Arbroath smokies
5 floz / 150 ml double cream
4 skinned, seeded & diced tomatoes
2 oz / 60g grated parmesan cheese
salt & pepper
lemon, cucumber or parsley for garnish

Method

Season 4 large individual ramekin dishes, divide the flaked fish between them & pour over the double cream.

Add one-quarter of the tomatoes to each dish & top with the cheese.

Bake in an oven preheated to 375°F/190°C/ gas 5 for 20 minutes, or place under a hot grill until bubbling.

Garnish with a twist of lemon or cucumber, or a sprig of parsley, & serve at once.

<u>Note</u>: if preferred, the cheese may be replaced with 3 oz / 85g breadcrumbs, fried in butter with a little crushed garlic.

Westmoreland raisin & nut pie with rum cream

Ingredients

12 oz / 340g sweet pastry (see page 153)

Filling
8 oz / 225g seedless raisins
1½ tbsp cornflour
3 oz / 85g sugar
pinch cinnamon
pinch salt
juice of ½ lemon
juice of ½ orange
2 oz / 60g chopped walnuts

Cream
10 fl oz / 300 ml double cream
2 fl oz / 60 ml dark rum
1 oz / 30g icing sugar

Method

Line an 8" / 20cm flan case with the sweet pastry & bake blind.

For the filling, simmer the raisins in a pan with a little water for 5 minutes.

Mix the cornflour, sugar, cinnamon & salt in a little cold water, add to the pan & cook until thickened.

Remove from the heat, add the lemon & orange juices, cool slightly & add the walnuts.

Spoon the mixture into the pastry case & chill.

For the cream, whisk the cream until thick, then fold in the rum & icing sugar.

To serve, cut the pie into wedges & top with cream.

The Cumbrian port of Whitehaven used to be a centre for the spice, sugar & rum trade with the West Indies, & smuggling was not unknown in the area. These ingredients have now been integrated into Cumbrian recipes.

THE BASICS
White Stock

Ingredients

5lb / 2.3kg veal bones, beef bones or
 chicken carcasses & giblets
8oz / 225g prepared carrot
4oz / 115g prepared onion
2oz / 60g prepared leek
1oz / 30g prepared celery
a few parsley stalks
1 sprig thyme
½ bay leaf
8pt / 5l litr water
salt

Method

 Ask the butcher to saw or chop the bones
into small pieces.
 Put the bones into a large saucepan,
cover with the cold water & a pinch of
salt, & bring slowly to the boil.
 Carefully remove the scum as it rises to
the surface.
 Add the vegetables & herbs, & simmer
gently for about 3 hours.
 Strain & use as required. The stock will
keep in the refrigerator for a couple of
days, or can be frozen in small quantities.
 Makes 7pt / 4 ltr.

JUS lié

Ingredients

4 lb / 1.8 kg raw veal & chicken bones, chopped
   into small pieces
4 oz / 115g diced carrot
3 oz / 85g diced onion
2 oz / 60g tomato purée
6 pt / 3.5 ltr cold water or white stock (see
   page 148)
1 small bayleaf
1 sprig thyme
3-4 parsley stalks
1 oz / 45g arrowroot

Method

Cook the bones until golden-brown in a
roasting tray in an oven preheated to
350°F / 180°C / gas 4, drain to remove excess
fat & place in a large saucepan.

Fry the carrot & onion in the roasting
tray until golden-brown, drain & add to the
bones with the tomato purée.

Add a little stock or water to the
roasting tray to loosen any sediment left
by the bones or vegetables, add this liquid
to the saucepan, cover with water or stock
& bring to the boil.

Remove any scum that rises to the
surface, reduce the heat, add the herbs &
simmer gently for 3 hours.

Strain the stock into a clean pan &
measure – you should be left with about
3 pt / 2.25 ltr.

Mix the arrowroot with a little cold
water or stock to form a smooth paste, then
add to the hot stock.

Reboil, stirring constantly, until it
thickens; cook for 2 minutes, strain & use
as required.

This sauce will keep in the refrigerator
for up to 3 days, but if a larger quantity
is made, only the amount needed immediately
should be thickened & the rest frozen in
small portions.

Brown stock

Ingredients

5 lb / 2.25 kg beef or veal bones, or some of
  each
8 oz / 225 g onion
8 oz / 225 g carrots
a little oil for frying
8 pt / 5 ltr water
2 oz / 60 g celery
3 or 4 sprigs parsley
1 sprig thyme
1 bayleaf

Method

Ask the butcher to saw or chop the bones
into small pieces.
  Put the bones into a roasting tray &
place in an oven preheated to 400°F / 200°C /
gas 6 for about 30 minutes, until well
browned.
  Cut the onion & carrot into 1" / 2 cm dice &
fry in a little oil.
  Put the onion, carrot & bones into a
large saucepan & cover with the cold water.
  Bring to the boil on top of the stove.
  Remove any scum as it rises to the
surface & add to the pan the celery & herbs
tied together.
  Simmer for at least 3 hours.
  Strain, remove fat & use as required.
Makes 7 pt / 4 ltr.
  The stock will keep in the refrigerator
for a couple of days, or can be frozen in
small quantities.

Fish stock

Ingredients

4 lb / 1.8 kg fish bones & trimmings
4 oz / 115 g sliced onion
3 or 4 parsley stalks
juice of 1 lemon
6 pt / 3.5 ltr. water
6 peppercorns

Method

Place the bones, trimmings, onion & parsley stalks in a large saucepan.

Add the lemon juice & water & bring quickly to the boil.

Carefully remove any scum as it rises.

Simmer for 15 minutes, add the peppercorns, then simmer for a further 10 minutes.

Do not add the peppercorns any earlier as this will cloud the stock.

Strain, reserve & use as required.

Makes 5 pt / 2.5 ltr.

This simple & quickly prepared stock can be used to make a fish sauce, or for poaching fish. Use only the bones of prime white fish such as sole, turbot, brill or whiting, avoiding those from oily fish such as salmon, herring or mackerel.

Puff Pastry

Ingredients

8oz / 225g unsalted butter
8oz / 225g strong white flour
pinch salt
3 fl oz / 90ml cold water
squeeze lemon juice

Method

Make sure the butter is of similar texture to the dough, ie, not too firm: if it is used straight from the refrigerator it will not spread evenly through the dough, thus spoiling the pastry.

Sift the flour & salt into a bowl, add the water & lemon juice & mix to a dough.

Knead until smooth & leave in a cool place for 30 minutes.

Cut a deep cross in the centre of the ball of dough & pull each point out from the centre.

Put the butter inside the dough & completely enclose by folding the flaps back over it.

With a floured rolling pin, roll the pastry into a rectangle, the long side 3 times the length of the short side, keeping the edges parallel.

One-third of the way along the long side, fold one-third of the pastry back over itself, & fold the remaining third over this.

Wrap in greaseproof paper & leave in a cool place for at least 20 minutes.

Roll into a rectangle as before, fold as before, wrap & rest as before.

Repeat twice more (ie, 4 turnings & foldings in all), always allowing a 20 minute resting period.

The final resting time should be for one hour, after which it is ready for use.

This yields 1 lb / 450g but larger quantities can be made & frozen.

Sweet pastry

Ingredients

12 oz / 340g plain flour
pinch salt
8 oz / 225g butter
2 oz / 60g castor sugar
4 oz / 115g beaten whole egg

Method

Sift the flour & salt into a basin.
Cut the butter into small pieces & rub
into the flour until the mixture resembles
fine breadcrumbs.
Dissolve the sugar in the beaten egg &
add to the flour & butter mixture.
Gently work the pastry to a smooth dough,
taking care not to handle it too much.
Allow the pastry to rest for at least 30
minutes before using.
This amount will line 2 flan rings of
8" / 20 cm in diameter.
The pastry will keep in the refrigerator
for a few days, or can be frozen.

Strudel pastry

Ingredients

14 oz / 400g strong flour
pinch salt
2 oz / 60g melted unsalted butter
1 beaten egg
5 fl oz / 150ml milk

Method

Sift the flour & salt into a bowl.
Add the melted butter, egg & milk & mix
to a smooth paste.
Knead well, just as you would for a bread
dough, cover & rest for 30 minutes, then
use as required.
Makes 2 strudels.

Tuile baskets

Ingredients

2 oz / 60g flour
2 oz / 60g icing sugar
1 egg white
2 oz / 60g melted & cooled unsalted butter

Method

Sift the flour & icing sugar into a bowl, beat in the egg white & stir in the cooled butter until well blended.

Place teaspoonfuls on a greased baking sheet, spread thinly to make circles of 4" / 10cm in diameter & bake in an oven preheated to 400°F / 200°C / gas 6 for 3-4 minutes.

Lift quickly off the baking sheet & cool over an upturned cup or mould to form a basket.

Makes 12-16.

Sugar syrup

Ingredients

1 pt / 500ml water
1 ½ lb / 680g sugar

Method

Boil the water & sugar in a heavy-based pan for 5 minutes, skimming as necessary.

Remove from the heat & pass through a conical sieve into a bowl.

Leave to cool & use as required.

Makes 2 pt / 1 ltr.

This syrup will keep for up to 2 weeks in a refrigerator.

Fresh custard

Ingredients

1 pt / 500 ml milk
4 egg yolks
2 oz / 60g castor sugar
few drops vanilla essence

Method

Put the milk in a saucepan & gradually bring to the boil.

Beat the egg yolks, sugar & vanilla essence in a basin until light & creamy.

When the milk is just about boiling, gradually pour it on to the egg mixture, whisking vigorously until fully incorporated.

Return the mixture to the saucepan & heat gently, stirring continuously, until it reaches a coating consistency.

On no account should the custard boil, as it might separate.

Strain through a fine sieve & keep warm until required.

Makes 1 pt / 500 ml.

This custard will not be as thick as one made with cornflour or custard powder.

Index by establishment

Morel's Restaurant (Jean-Yves & Mary-Anne Morel, 25-27 Lower Street, Haslemere, Surrey GU27 2NY Tel: (0428) 51462 p 96

Ninety Park Lane, Grosvenor House Hotel, Park Lane, London W1A 3AA Tel: (01) 499 6363 p 98

Park Hotel (Francis Brennan), Kenmare, Co Kerry, Republic of Ireland Tel: (010 - 353 64) 41200 p 100

Pebbles Restaurant (David & Susan Cavalier), Pebble Lane, Aylesbury, Buckinghamshire HP20 2HJ Tel: (0296) 86622 p 102

Plumber Manor (The Prideaux-Brune Family), Sturminster Newton, Dorset DT10 2AF Tel: (0258) 72507 p 104

Pool Court Restaurant (Michael Gill), Pool-in-Wharfedale, nr Otley, West Yorkshire LS21 1EH Tel: (0532) 842288 p 106

Portsonachan Hotel (Christopher & Caroline Trotter), South Loch-aweside, by Dalmally, Argyll PA33 1BL Tel: (086 63) 224 p 110

Le Poussin (Alex & Caroline Aitken), 57/59 Brookley Road, Brockenhurst, Hampshire SO42 7RB Tel: (0590) 23063 p 112

Read's Restaurant (Keith Read), 152 Old Brompton Road, London SW5 0BE Tel: (01) 373 2445 p 114

Restaurant Nineteen (Stephen Smith & Robert Barbour), Belvedere Hotel, 19 North Park Road, Heaton, Bradford, West Yorkshire BD9 4NT Tel: (0274) 492559 p 116

Restaurant Roger Burdell, The Manor House, Sparrow Hill, Loughborough LE11 1BT Tel: (0509) 231813 p 120

Roger's Restaurant (Roger & Alena Pergl-Wilson), 4 High Street, Windermere, Cumbria LA23 1AF Tel: (096 62) 4954 p 124

Rule's Restaurant (John Mayhew & Jeremy Mogford) 35 Maiden Lane London WC2E 7LB Tel: (01) 836 5314 p 126

Sharrow Bay Hotel (Francis Coulson & Brian Sack), Howtown Road, Ullswater, Penrith, Cumbria CA10 2LZ Tel: (085 36) 483 p 128

Le Soufflé, Hotel Inter-Continental, 1 Hamilton Place, Hyde Park Corner, London W1V 0QY Tel: (01) 409 3131 p 132

La Tante Claire (Pierre Koffmann), 68 Royal Hospital Road, London SW3 4LP Tel: (01) 352 6045 p 136

Thornbury Castle (Maurice & Carol Taylor), Thornbury, nr Bristol, Avon BS12 1HH Tel: (0454) 412647 p 138

The Walnut Tree Inn (Franco & Ann Taruschio), Llandewi Skirrid, Abergavenny, Gwent, Wales NP7 8AW Tel: (0873) 2797 p 140

The Waterside Inn (Michel Roux), Ferry Road, Bray-on-Thames, Berkshire SL6 2AT Tel: (0628) 20691 p 142

White Moss House (Sue & Peter Dixon), Rydal Water, Grasmere, Cumbria LA22 9SE Tel: (096 65) 295 p 146

Homewood Park

Index by recipe

GAME

Pheasant: Breast & leg of pheasant with green peppercorns p 33
  Pheasant with winter vegetables & pine kernels p 38
Pigeon: Pigeon breasts with red wine, bacon & foie gras p 28
  Pigeonneaux au coulis de pêches p 142
Quail: Pot-roast quail with Stilton mousse & muscat grape sauce p102
Smoked quail: Smoked breasts of quail with mange-tout pears & a
  truffle & herb sauce p 64
Rabbit: Paupiettes of wild rabbit with lovage & mustard p 30
  Sauté of rabbit with apples & Calvados p116
Venison: Venison noisettes with marc de Bourgogne p 53

MEAT

Beef: A little idea from Japan with beef & ginger p 58
  Bresaola p 140
  Clare Hilti's Hungarian goulash p 106
  Fillet of beef with rosemary & mustard p35
Foie gras: Terrine of leeks & foie gras p112
Kidneys: Pan-fried veal kidneys on creamed endive with a honey &
  lemon sauce p 92
  Rognons de veau rôtis, poêlée d'escargots, & sauce vin rouge
  au persil & à la Chartreuse verte p84
Lamb: Fillet of lamb with fresh mint cream sauce p 26
  Sauté of lamb with red peppers, basil & coppa p 4
Liver: Calves' liver with avocado p108
  Sauté of calves' liver with whiskey & tarragon p 10
Pork: Fillet of pork with spinach, wild mushrooms & port wine
  sauce p 68
  Loin or shoulder of pork with red cabbage p 120
Veal: Medallions of veal with port wine sauce & onion marmalade p 130
  Paupiettes of veal stuffed with chicken & sage mousse p 12

POULTRY

Chicken: Delicate ragoût of chicken & mussels in basil &
  Pernod sauce p66
  Les pilons de volaille à la vapeur au basilic et aux ravioles p 134
  Roast chicken with tarragon, brandy & cream p 14
  Stuffed breast of chicken flamed in Pernod p138
Duck: Confit de canard au chou vert et aux pignons de pin p 20
  Stuffed duckling with lentils in cream & garlic p 62

SAVOURY SOUFFLES

Soufflé aux épinards, sauce anchois p78
Soufflé suissesse p 46

SHELLFISH

Crab: Crab soufflé suissesse p16
  Tomato & fresh crab ring p 11
Dublin Bay prawns: Dublin Bay prawns with garlic & herb butter p18
Langoustines: Jardinière de langoustines p9
Mussels: Boudin de moules au beurre d'ail p96
Scallops: Princess scallops with saffron p 110
  Scallop mousse with beurre blanc p 36

SOUPS

Fresh mussel soup p101
Hawthorn & cucumber soup p6
North Sea fish soup p 52

VEGETABLES & SALADS

Gratin of potatoes & Jerusalem artichokes p40
Salad of English ewes' milk cheese, tomato & herbs p 126
Warm vegetable salad with grilled Yarg p 114
Wild fungi in pastry p 81
Winter salad p 41

Acknowledgements

Many thanks to all the chefs who took time out of their busy schedules to send in recipes, & in some cases to discuss them at length on the telephone. Apologies to those whose recipes we could not include in this volume owing to space & time restrictions.

Dishes researched, cooked, eaten, written up, drawn, quantified, computerised & edited by the Alfresco team: Chris Ackerman-Eveleigh, Philip Diment, Angela Nicholson & Sally Simpson, assisted by Barbara Baran, Janet Fahy & Don MacPherson.

Roy Ackerman has recently written 'The Ackerman Guide' to the best restaurants & hotels in the British Isles, published by Penguin. The book has been well received by both the catering trade & the public as an 'insider's guide', challenging the existing publications with its positive approach.

Roy Ackerman has been involved in the catering industry for many years, starting in the trade as a commis chef, then working in all departments of the kitchen as an apprentice both in England & Europe. He opened his first restaurant in Oxford in 1976 & within three years had opened three more.

He is a well-known figure within the catering trade: in 1985 he was awarded the Special Prize at the Caterer & Hotelkeeper Awards & elected a Fellow of the Hotel & Catering Institute. As Chairman of the Restaurateurs Association of Great Britain he was a principal instigator of the licensing reform bill. He is also co-chairman of the Henley Festival of Music & the Arts.

Roy Ackerman has originated & presented a six-part television documentary, 'The Chef's Apprentice': a history of food networked by Independent Television.